Signs of Hope

Signs of Hope

Archbishop David Hope

CONTINUUM
London and New York

Continuum
The Tower Building, 11 York Road London SE1 7NX
370 Lexington Avenue, New York, NY 10017–6503

© 2001 Continuum International Publishing in association
with *The Tablet*

Text © 2001 David Hope

First published 2001

British Library Cataloguing-in-Publication Data
A catalogue record for this book is available from the British Library.

ISBN 0 8264 5688 X

Typeset by YHt Ltd, London

Printed and bound in Great Britain by Biddles Ltd,
Guildford and King's Lynn

Contents

vi

Introduction

The Preface to the Declaration of Assent is for the Church of England a key document. It is the subject of Canonical provision – C15 of the Declaration of Assent. It sets out fundamental statements about the Church of England's own self-understanding. It testifies to the claim that it is 'part of the One Holy Catholic and Apostolic Church', that it 'professes the faith uniquely revealed in the Holy Scriptures and set forth in the Catholic Creeds' – this 'deposit' of faith to be proclaimed afresh in each generation. It concludes by posing the challenge of bringing the grace and truth of Christ, and making Him known, to this generation.

In other words, how is it possible to relate those saving events of the past, as evidenced by the writers of the New Testament, concerning the words and works of Jesus Christ, His life, death and resurrection, to the fast-moving world of today? How is the unchanging truth of the Gospel to be understood and communicated in an ever-changing world?

In a previous collection of sermons and addresses – *Living the Gospel* – now the title of a mission intiative throughout the whole Diocese of York, I attempted to reflect something of this challenge.

Athough now in a different context, the same endeavour continues as Archbishop of York. Indeed one of the key dimensions of any episcopal ministry must be the apostolic task of teaching and nurturing – not in any vacuum, but rather engaging with the issues of the day both in the Church and in the world. This I have sought to do through this present volume.

The collection straddles not only a new century but also a new millennium; a time when, generally, the 'established' churches of the West are in decline in terms of membership, yet, paradoxically, the surveys tell us that there is a considerable interest in things spiritual. More people are turning to prayer, and a substantial majority continue to profess a belief in God.

Attempting to discern the signs of the times amid paradox and complexity admits to no easy or quick fixes. Moreover, there will always be the temptation either to abandon the tradition altogether – that which has been from the beginning – or so formalize it with a fundamentalism that admits of no interrogation whatever, that it becomes difficult, if not impossible, to chart any way forward.

Signs of Hope sets before us another way: evangelization as engagement – a readiness to engage with the Gospel in very different settings and, hopefully, to make connections; the sort of connections which will lead to further thought and reflection, inspire greater confidence and encourage all on their journey of both faith and life.

One of the great privileges I have as Archbishop is the way in which it is possible to meet and mix with so many people as I respond to invitations not only throughout the Diocese of York but also in the Northern Province and well beyond. I continue to be astonished by the number of invitations I receive quite outside and beyond the Church itself and which, wherever possible, I seek to accept. For always, in whatever setting or context, there is the opportunity to meet, to engage, to discuss and to explore; to encourage others in their own search for faith, for meaning, and for God.

My hope is that this volume will encourage and deepen the faith and life of all who read it. There are signs enough of disillusion and pessimism. But that cannot be the whole picture. There are equally signs of faith and life and hope born of my own experience as a Bishop, and emerging from people and communities, as 'Church' and for whom Jesus Christ – the same yesterday, today and for ever – is at the heart of their lives as they seek to continue to be faithful to that inheritance of faith as expressed in the Preface to the Declaration of Assent, and who, in so many differing and varied situations and contexts, are clearly and evidently bringing the grace and truth of Christ, and making Him known, to this generation. This book must be an appreciation of their ministry and mission and is offered as a tribute to them.

One

Sermon for the enthronement at York Minster

Friday, 8 December 1995

'The Lord has done great things for me; and holy is His name'
(Luke 1.49)

The greatness and the holiness of God are surely nowhere
more evident than here in this Church of St Peter in which we
gather this afternoon. Its origins take us into the earliest days
of the Christian mission in this land, recalling the names of
Eborius and Paulinus, Cedd and Wilfrid, as well as names of
more recent times – Temple and Ramsey, and yet more
recently still, Coggan, Blanch and Habgood. York Minster tells
its own story – the history of Christianity in northern England,
the story of sinners and saints, of fire and pillage, of subterfuge
and discord, a story in which Christian faith and purpose, ever
fragile and precarious, has nevertheless flourished. It is a
place, too, for which – as I hope with every Yorkshireman good
and true – I have always had a personal and special affection,
though I have to admit that when I was first brought to York as
a youngster, Mallard in the railway sheds held rather more
interest than Walter de Grey in the Minster!

The greatness and the holiness of God is surely pre-
eminently evident in the mystery of that which has been
accomplished in Mary. This young woman of Nazareth,
acclaimed Theotokos – God-bearer – by the Church, conceives

in her womb and brings forth Emmanuel – God with us and alongside us, God among us forever and always – holy is His name.

Here is an acclamation, too, which each of us can echo as we reflect upon the great things God has done for us in His Church and in His world. I rejoice and am grateful that so many of you from the Diocese, the Province, my former Dioceses of Wakefield and London and yet further afield still, have been able to come and be with me for this splendid, yet awesome, occasion. I rejoice, too, that our sisters and brothers in Christ from other denominations and Churches are here with us, a clear sign that we are pilgrims together. As we look towards the new millennium – the celebration of which marks above and before all else the birth of Jesus Christ – we certainly need each other, to be with and alongside each other in Christian witness, service and mission. Today, I want to make very clear my own continuing commitment to this task.

I am deeply conscious, both of the honour and of the responsibility with which I am now entrusted as Archbishop of York. Yet, as with any ministry in the Church, it can only be effective if it is exercised for the building up of the Church and its mission in the world, and in concert with the many other gifts which God has entrusted to His Church. We are all called – ordained and lay – as members of one body, belonging together, working together as one body – as ourselves God-bearers, like the Blessed Virgin whose conception we celebrate today – bearers of the Good News of Jesus Christ, crucified and risen.

It is right to pause and reflect upon our roots and our history at a time when, while there is much to celebrate in the Church, there is also a good deal of anxiety and uncertainty. A new Synod, a new millennium, structures and finance, family life and human sexuality, management and ministry; when perhaps old certainties seem not to be quite so certain as once they were, and where even our best efforts appear to elicit only a modest response. As we seek a way forward, we need to draw upon and learn from the insights and wisdom of the past as the inspiration for the future. For, certainly, the context in which the early Christian mission in these parts was prosecuted was hardly more congenial than the present. Yet it was only through the persistent and often infuriatingly unconventional ways of those whose names I have already recalled, that Christian England came to be shaped and formed.

There were no synods as we know and experience them. Or, if there were, they chose not to take much notice of them. There were bishops and there were kings, but often that made little difference. What there was in these God-bearers was a fearlessness, a boldness, an energy and a zeal for the things of God; a missionary extravagance, which was incapable of being hemmed in by the four walls of any church, or any committee or board or council, even an Archbishops' Council! Their missionary enterprise flourished best in its risk-taking venturesomeness, going out and about, from place to place, engaging with every kind of person and place, not because they saw themselves on any conversion trail, but because they had a vision. They were the God-bearers they were only because they had been both seized of and possessed by a vision of God, the greatness and the holiness of God, a vision whole and complete It caught up all people and all things in the God who had become incarnate of the Blessed Virgin and had taken upon Himself our feeble, frail and fallen human nature, so that what He had created after His own image and likeness might yet more wonderfully be restored by Him, in Him, and through Him. Yes, whoever you are, whatever your circumstances, each is encouraged this day to sing with Mary's Magnificat – 'The Lord has done great things for me, holy is His name.'

Now, just in case you may be thinking that I am suffering a bad attack of golden-age-itis, one thing we can learn from the past is the need for greater reflection. We allow ourselves too often to be satisfied with the superficial, too addicted to the quick fix, to short-termism. We have too short an attention span to allow God to sow his seeds of faith and hope in reflection and contemplation. Bede writes of King Edwin, baptized at this very place, that he was 'by nature a wise and prudent man, and often sat alone in silence for long periods, turning over in his mind what he should do'. Reflection and reflectiveness – taking the long view – is a quality which we need to recover as much for our own human well-being and flourishing, as for the Church's. We need space for God's holiness to dawn, for the vision of God to seize us and to possess us and to make us whole. 'God's speech is framed by silence' is a memorable phrase I heard in a sermon recently.

It was to a vision of God's greatness and holiness that Mary was responding, and so too were those of whom I have been speaking. Furthermore, it was a vision of God's beauty and God's splendour not tarnished by any hint of churchiness and religiosity. For here were men and women, who through their learning and their prayer, their faith and contemplation, were able to see a world transformed – truly God's kingdom come on earth as it is in heaven – a kingdom of righteousness of justice and of truth. It is, yes, a vision of faith, but it is a moral vision too, where the inward and the spiritual is bodied forth into the outward and the visible, into the practical and the pastoral and the behavioural. There is a consistency and a coherence here precisely because God is seen as the *fons et origo* of every aspect of human life and society.

Amidst the complexity and paradox of the many questions which press in upon our modern world, coherence of vision is to be found not in the following of a book, a theory or even a creed, but in the following of a person, Jesus Christ, the same yesterday, today and for ever. And so I urge the Church, like Mary, to remain steadfast and faithful in following Christ, and with the writer of the letter to the Hebrews, 'to run with perseverance the race that is set before us, looking to Jesus the pioneer and perfecter of our faith, who for the joy that was set before him, endured the Cross, despising the shame, and is now seated at the right hand of the throne of God'.

'The Lord has done great things for me; and holy is His name.'

The Lord has done great things for us – holy is His name. To Him be the glory for ever and ever. Amen.

Two

Diocese of Manchester – Celebration Eucharist to launch Jubilee 97

Thursday, 5 December 1996

'Say to them ... the kingdom of God has come near to you' (Luke 10.9)

Tonight as you embark upon a year of Jubilee – a year of celebration and triumphal shout, a year of freedom and liberation, a year of restoration and renewal – we give thanks for the vision, foresight and dedication of those who 150 years ago saw to it that Manchester was on the map not only commercially but also ecclesiastically. It was on the occasion when one of my predecessors, as Archbishop of York, William Temple, about to become Bishop of Manchester, that the then Prime Minister, Lloyd George, wrote to him – 'The Diocese is one of great importance, situated as it is in the centre of a large business community and comprising a great industrial population.' Not to be outdone, the then Archbishop of Canterbury was even more eulogistic – 'The vacant post is one of the greatest in the Church of England or perhaps in the whole Church of Christ, alike in the possibilities and the weight of its burden.' And I dare say that Bishop Christopher would echo this last phrase embracing both the boundless possibilities and the immensities of the burden.

It was in the wake of the great industrial revolution and in view of the burgeoning population in the North West, together with the establishment of Manchester and Salford as a focal point of world trade, and the growth of other centres – Bolton, Bury, Oldham, Rochdale and so on – you will know them better than I – that moves were made towards the creation of the new Diocese of Manchester. Eventually, the diocese was established – a huge diocese – the whole of Lancashire and more, subsequently to be divided. This ancient collegiate Church of St Mary, St Denys and St George became a very appropriate and fitting cathedral for the new see.

So what are our priorities for ministry and mission as this year of Jubilee begins? First, surely, there is celebration, of our shared faith and belonging. The story of the diocese from its beginning until now is a remarkable story of the workings of God's mercy and grace. We celebrate the blessings of belonging to this Church of England – a Church which, against all the odds, has remained both in the city and the countryside; a Church which in rapidly changing times, conditions and circumstances remains faithful to its calling as part of the One, Holy, Catholic and Apostolic Church – a household of faith built upon the foundation of the apostles and prophets, with Jesus Christ himself as the chief cornerstone. Because of the historic context and the way in which, inextricably, Church and nation have emerged in this land, there is, thankfully, the perception still that we are not here for ourselves, but rather to serve others – a Church which is available to all and for all.

The parochial system, which is the expression and embodiment of this availability locally in a whole variety of ways and places, is still to be cherished and valued. It is the backbone of our Church. We should be doing all we can in ensuring in each diocese and in the Church a vision for mission and evangelism, a clear strategy in which it is the job of the centre to support and encourage the local churches, places, communities, sectors themselves – rich and poor, large and small, mutually supportive of each other – with a real generosity of spirit; and where, through worship and prayer, teaching and nurture, care and service we continue to make known the glorious Gospel of God's saving work in Jesus Christ for all. And here in the North we are rightly proud of our tradition of community – of what might best be described as a 'nosy neighbourliness' – a sign at its best that we do have a care and a concern for and about everyone.

And it will very often be in the ordinary and the unspectacular, in the humdrum of the everyday things, the sheer slog of seeking to remain faithful – all that which goes quite unreported, which never makes the headlines because on the whole it actually is good news, the very environment right where the Church is – right where you are, where the fresh yet fragile shoots of new life and hope and promise appear day by day.

Nor do I speak lightly or without a real awareness of the tremendous difficulties and obstacles faced by every diocese in the land – finance, buildings, structures, resources – and this diocese is no exception. But then as the saying goes – Where there's a will, there's a way.

Now it hardly behoves me, a Yorkshireman, to be saying in the heart of Lancashire, given those sterling northern qualities of grit, determination and stickability, that there is a lack either of a will or of a way, even though I do still wonder about the remark by two churchwardens I heard recently in one parish – 'You know Bishop it's our inertia that actually keeps us going!'

So let us celebrate the blessings of belonging: always holding before us the sheer wonder and splendour and glory of the God who is seeking ever to transform His Church, our society, the entire nation. Let us not be so hugely diverted by structures and strategies that we fail first and foremost to humble ourselves before the eternal and living God who alone can create a new spirit within us and who already has taken our human nature to himself in Christ and set before us the way, the truth and the life.

The second clear Jubilee theme is that of liberation and freedom: good news to the poor, the setting at liberty of those who are oppressed; reconciliation and remission; the whole social dimension of the Gospel. Here in Manchester you have had some weighty characters and leaders in your bishops. Both your second and fourth bishops, Fraser and Knox, keenly involved themselves in education, the former establishing the Diocesan Board of Education, the latter leading a demonstration of some ten thousand to protest to Parliament at a proposed Education Bill which if passed would have sounded the death knell for religious instruction and Church teaching from the school timetable. And then there is the magisterial contribution of William Temple to our Church's social teaching or the outspoken attacks of Bishop Warman on the new paganisms of Soviet Communism and German Nazism. I can still very well remember a number of forthright contributions in the House of Bishops as well as in the House of Lords by Bishop Booth-Clibborn.

The 'common good' was as much a theme of that landmark report in our Church – *Faith in the City* – as it is of the recent and timely statement by the Roman Catholic bishops. Both of them begin with God, the divine society of the Blessed Trinity, and the radical, relevant and far-reaching implications which a seemingly arcane theology has for the way in which our society is to be ordered. The fact that God has not just an interest in but also reveals himself through the ordering of creation and society is a common theme which runs through-out the Scriptures – both Old and New Testaments – and on into a long line of Christian social thought from Augustine to the present day. And whilst certainly it may be argued that Jesus' teaching on the kingdom sets before us a pattern of human relationships which can only be fully realized in the age to come, there is nevertheless the persistent implication that these can at least in some measure be experienced in the present. And other values, such as freely given mutual service, care for the weak and vulnerable and marginalized, the overcoming of racial and social barriers, are undoubtedly present in other parts of the New Testament and have an equal claim on our thinking and action. As *Faith in the City* comments: it is the elaboration of these elements into an actual system of social and political life which has occupied the minds of English Christians from Thomas More to the Christian reformers of the nineteenth and twentieth centuries.

And that same challenge is before us still, not least as we look towards a General Election; to weigh seriously the implications for today of Jesus' own forthright statement that the kingdom of God has come near you. And it is as much a challenge to ourselves as it is to our politicians. The Roman Catholic bishops conclude – 'it is about a reclamation of public life from utilitarian expediency and the pursuit of self interest ...' – for the common good. It has been enormously encouraging even in my brief time with you here in the diocese, to meet people and to visit places where manifestly such signs of the kingdom of God are clearly evident and where often against all the odds there is life and there is hope for the future.

A third and concluding Jubilee theme is that of restoration and renewal in the first place within ourselves. Our future together begins here and now with each one of us and that conversion of heart and mind and soul begun in baptism and by God's mercy and grace alone, continually extended and deepened in this eucharistic mystery in which we celebrate the life of the age to come – God's kingdom come among us, as in heaven.

Earlier this year, this city was dealt a devastating blow; a grievous wound to its very heart. So evil and potentially life threatening an act perpetrated in your city centre has served only to galvanize further the determination of all, so that rather than allowing yourselves to be overcome by evil, you will overcome evil with good. For from the destruction and devastation of former buildings a new scheme will arise, already a much heralded transformation of the heart of the city. And such an exciting project engages the support of us all with its promise of an altogether brighter and better future. Yet the psalmist of old both reminds and warns us, 'except the Lord build the city ...' – those words speak to us all whoever we may be, facing us starkly again with the need for that personal renewal and restoration of life and a readiness ourselves to be committed with others in ensuring the partnerships and relationships which are based not so much on our own individual wants and needs and rights but on an awareness of the common good and the Lord's command that we should love our neighbour as ourselves.

Believing and belonging; liberation and freedom; restoration and renewal – profound and powerful themes for this year of Jubilee and with potentially more onerous tasks yet before us for the sake of the Gospel of Christ.

I think therefore I can do no better than to conclude with those same words which my predecessor here in the See of Manchester and in York, Archbishop William Temple himself, concluded his own enthronement address in this very cathedral seventy-five years ago this year – 'We go forward together – not without stumbling, not without weariness – but always towards the loving welcome that awaits us in our Father's home, where the conflicts which now beset the earth will have vanished, where self-seeking cannot find entrance, where misery gives place to joy and quarrelling to peace, because self is either sacrificed or forgotten in the realization of the love of God.' So as daily we pray that God's kingdom may come on earth as it is in heaven, also we go and say to them 'The kingdom of God has come near you.'

Three

National Pilgrimage to the Shrine of Our Lady of Walsingham

Monday, 27 May 1996

'You shall be my witnesses ... to the end of the earth' (Acts 1.8)

Making my way to Walsingham today I remembered the first time I came here in 1954. I still have the booklet I bought then, written by Father Hope Patten, which tells the story of Mary's Shrine. Never then did I for one moment imagine I would be here before you today in the archepiscopal office to which I have been appointed and with which I have been entrusted. In those early days of which Father Hope Patten speaks, an archbishop may have been much more hesitant of making any appearance, after a founding Guardian, in one of the more heated controversies of the day, had expressed the strong view of the then Archbishop of York — 'I cannot conceive anything more splendid than that Your Grace should be executed on Tower Hill. Nothing but the martyrdom of the Archbishop can save the Church of England. I crave the honour of it for you and that I should be there, that I might plunge my kerchief in your blood.' No doubt some of you may harbour similar thoughts and desires from time to time, perhaps all of the time, over quite different yet equally controversial matters!

So what is it that has kept us coming here to Walsingham year by year? What is it that down the ages and over the years has drawn countless pilgrims, young and old, rich and poor, high and low, to England's Nazareth? There is this National Pilgrimage, the 'big do' event which we all appreciate and enjoy. And it is entirely right that we should enjoy such a day together. There are the quieter occasions too – times of thanksgiving and joy as well as of personal anguish and trouble – all reflected as we make our way here and echoed so movingly at Shrine prayers every evening; and once here, like Mary, we ponder on the deep mystery of God's love for us, just as we are, in the gift of his only son. There is something of a sense of 'coming home' to Walsingham; a coming home which one day will be eternally.

What then is it to which we bear witness in coming here to Walsingham? The truth of the incarnation sets before us a world 'charged with the grandeur of God'. Yes, the wonder and the beauty of God's creation is here all around us and yet the environment is increasingly threatened by greed and misuse. If we are truly to celebrate the glory of God's creation then we have a responsibility to ensure the safeguarding of our environment for generations yet to come. Just as God entrusted His son to the arms of the Blessed Mother, so the world has been entrusted to humanity, not to squander and to plunder but to tend and cherish, to care for and to nurture. And, no, I am not becoming a trendy green, yet I do believe that the witness of Walsingham is altogether more profound and far-reaching than perhaps we even realize. Walsingham is in the first place a witness to God and His initiative in creation and to His act of re-creation in Christ.

We are witnesses then to the God who created us and in Christ redeemed us. At the heart of Walsingham is the foundational and fundamental truth of the Christian religion: the incarnation of the Son of God. It is the witness to that astounding claim that in Jesus Christ the eternal and ever-lasting God has spoken his final and definitive word, that in Jesus Christ God has revealed himself uniquely. The apostolic preaching was not only folly and a stumbling-block to those who heard it; it was nothing less than sheer scandal. Yet this is the faith of the Church which comes to us from the apostles, the faith in which we celebrate this Eucharist today, in which we remain steadfast, and indeed rejoice. Complacency, however, is dangerous. We live in a world where many people do not know about Jesus Christ. They have never heard because they have never been told. And I am not talking here about people in other lands. I am talking about people in our parishes, deaneries and dioceses in our own land. For far too many the name of Jesus is more by way of a curse than it is a blessing.

There is an urgent need for more effective teaching of the basic truths of our faith, for catechesis. The word itself implies not only a thoroughness and enthusiasm for what is being taught, but that the very teaching has a sort of resounding, ringing effect which not only re-echoes back to the teacher, but actually resounds, rings out in the very life and style of the individual and community so catechized; such teaching setting out a clear basis for our values, standards and style of life. It is a huge encouragement to know that the Shrine has taken an initiative in teaching and nurture with a particular emphasis on young people.

This enterprise is the responsibility of us all. It must be firmly rooted in the worshipping life of the Church – 'theology with church bells' Michael Ramsey once called it – where Christian faith is caught as much by exposure and experience in the context of worship and prayer as it is in the more formal setting of instruction. How many of you present here have not experienced again and again the converting and renewing power of the liturgy – Christ present and active in the sacramental life of the Church? From the earliest times – and the New Testament itself provides ample evidence of this – there have been differences and divisions with varying degrees of virulence and invective. Differences among us remain, both within our own church and in relation to other churches and denominations, and whilst we ought never to minimize those things which keep us apart, it is equally vital for the sake of the Christian mission in our land that we seek to make common cause on the very truth on which this Shrine of Our Lady of Walsingham is established – the incarnation.

Walsingham remains what it is and has been and always will be – a sign and symbol of the Catholic revival in the Church of England. The Chapter of Guardians is clear that it has no intention of handing this Anglican Shrine over to any other ecclesial body and that we are now beginning the process of election to fill the vacant places both of priest and lay Guardians who are in good standing in the Church to which the Shrine is affiliated, namely the Church of England. We have a new Master of Guardians, Father Peter Cobb – we welcome him and assure him of our prayers and our support. And in so welcoming him we must also express our gratitude to Christopher Colven whose association with the Shrine has stretched over many years, not only more recently as Master but as Guardian and Administrator and, like each of us, and really most importantly of all, as a pilgrim.

The tensions and difficulties we have faced recently might well be interpreted as a disturbing power of the Holy Spirit to alert us to fresh and new ways of sustaining and nurturing relationships between the Roman Catholic Church and the Church of England, and where, in particular here in Walsingham, the paradox of the one domain which encompasses the two Shrines is perhaps already a sign and a foretaste of that day when the, for now, imperfect communion which we share will be brought to the fullness of perfection in and through Him the one Lord and Saviour of us all. Meanwhile if the healing, reconciliation and renewal which is at the very heart of our witness here in Walsingham is to have about it any reality at all, it must be in the patient forbearance we have one with another as we seek not to have our own selfish and partial wills and ways, but the true discernment of God's will and God's way. After all, we are not strangers but rather pilgrims together – pilgrims together along Walsingham's way, united in baptism in the One Lord and Saviour whose kingdom we proclaim – a kingdom of justice, righteousness, peace and love.

Most important and vital of all we need to remember that as with the fundamental parochial principle of the Church of England, the Shrine is open to all and for all. Our Blessed Lady holds out, offers, her incarnate Son and Lord to any and all who would see Jesus. That witness remains and it is yours and mine too; to hold out Jesus Christ, to make Him known – to make His name glorious in our land.

So then we go from Walsingham into the world which God has entrusted to us, strengthened in faith and renewed in the power of the Holy Spirit. We can have no illusions about the challenge which is before us as we seek to make Christ known, to tell and to live the Gospel message in an anxious, troubled and increasingly confrontational world. The witness to which the Church is called remains a martyrdom. Not the martyrdom of bloodshedding, but the martyrdom of obedience and faithfulness, patterned for us in the Blessed Mother; the martyrdom of not being conformed to this world, but rather ourselves and our world being caught up into the transforming recreation of all things effected by God through the incarnation of His only Son, and in the power of His Holy Spirit – a new Pentecost, which is both our confidence in the present and our hope for the future.

Four

Ecumenical Service on the occasion of the visit of the President of Ireland

York Minster – Friday, 7 June 1996

'I bow my knees before the Father' (Ephesians 3.14)

And this is precisely what hundreds and thousands have done in this place down the ages and across the years, from that moment when Paulinus here in York preached the Gospel and baptized Edwin, King of Northumbria, just as two hundred years earlier Patrick had preached the same Gospel before the pagan chieftains at Tara. York Minster tells the story of these northern parts, the story of a people in health and prosperity and peace; a people, as well, in adversity and strife and war. Conflict has never been far from the currency of human life and in this place both victor and vanquished have been laid to rest and thus found their common destiny before the judgement seat of God; equally here are to be found the promise and the presence of forgiveness, reconciliation and peace.

In welcoming President Robinson today, together with His Royal Highness the Duke of York and all of you in this congregation as the latest in a long line of pilgrims, we all come here in the first place in worship and in prayer. This Minster by its very grandeur and presence gives us a sense of humility and awe before God. Paul's exhortation is not simply to a polite and gentle bending of the knee. Our human situation is far too precarious and serious for that; it is rather to a prostration of the whole person, the laying of our whole selves before God in outward and visible acknowledgement of our desperate need both of God's mercy and of God's grace, especially at this time, when the hopes and longings of so many are tempered by memories of past failure. Furthermore, such an act of kneeling in prayer, prostrate before God and each other, is a recognition of the fact of our humanness and that as a consequence our views and insights will necessarily be limited, partial and imperfect.

The agonized prayer of Jesus, prostrate before His Father in Gethsemane, which formed part of our second reading this morning, is highly significant. It is properly and powerfully invoked as the imperative for Christian unity, but never a unity which is an end in itself – 'may they all be one ... that the world may believe'. This is what we hope and long for; this is our prayer and our vision. Yet is such a vision deliverable, given our human condition, our fallen and fallible human nature; the 'envy, hatred, malice and all uncharitableness' of which our Litany speaks and which is in some measure to be found in everyone of us? What chance is there of any progress at all? Left to our own devices and desires the prospects are not encouraging. Yet the Scriptures are clear, even confident – 'with God nothing is impossible'.

Prayer and action are inseparable. The dialogue of relationship, trust and reconciliation which is established both in our speaking and in our listening as we pray before God, is to be patterned in the dialogue of relationship, trust and reconciliation which we pursue with friend and foe alike. The Chief Rabbi reminds us that dialogue has been one of the great religious achievements of the past half-century – 'It has promoted a new mood of mutual understanding and respect. But its work has hardly begun.' 'Religion,' he writes (and here he cites Ireland, Bosnia, the Middle East and elsewhere), 'is still used to defend ethnic or national rivalry, and it still claims human sacrifices.'

If the utterances of religious and political leaders are to have about them any authentic currency, and not simply remain the platitudes they sometimes seem to be, then much more still needs to be done at every level to ensure that an altogether more purposeful shift in perception and understanding takes place on all sides which includes the possibility of establishing a truly fresh culture, environment and ethos in which the dialogue of relationship, trust and reconciliation can be more fervently pursued. Yes, there are memories; the deep, searing and painful hurts, resentments and hatreds which cannot and will not be forgotten and eradicated. We bring our past with us. It cannot be undone. To forget the past, to wipe it out as though it had never been, is dubious both on the grounds of human psychology, and even more on grounds of Christian theology. As Christians, of whatever tradition, we are bound to believe and to teach that the way to heal the wounds of history is not to forget but to repent. There is a direct and inescapable relationship between repentance and reconciliation. And is not this very relationship an already established foundational fact not only of Ireland's memory but of its life-story, highly relevant for these present times? It has been from the very beginning exemplified for us in the life of Patrick, himself having been captured at an early age by a party of Irish raiders and carried off into slavery as a tender of flocks on the mountains of Antrim or Mayo. In the six years of his captivity his nominal Christian faith was exchanged for an active belief: he relates in his 'Confessions' how he learned to pray on the hillsides. Eventually, having escaped to Britain, he at once began to train for the priesthood, with a view to returning to preach Christian truth to his Irish captors. He did exactly that. The Irish chieftains listened to their escaped slave. They did not hinder him. Rather, and remarkably, bearing in mind the barbarity of the times, they forgave him; the conversion of Ireland was achieved without martyrs. Patrick's forgiveness of his Irish masters, and their forgiveness of him, indicated a shift of ground by both parties and an authentic celebration of reconciliation: nothing less than the conversion of a whole people. And Irish Christianity, in the Dark Ages, became one of the brightest beacons of faith in Europe.

In our own day, Nelson Mandela in his autobiography, at the beginning of the chapter 'Beginning to Hope', reminds us that the graph of improvement is never steady. 'Progress was halting, and typically accompanied by setbacks. An advancement might take years to win, and then be rescinded in a day.

We would push the rock up the hill, only to have it tumble down again.' How many negotiators for reconciliation and peace in whatever context experience exactly that. Yet from the Christian perspective it is vital that in spite of all the setbacks such dialogue continues to be pursued. It can be a long and dispiriting business and even when there seems to be little possibility of achieving anything at all, not only the persistence in prayer but also the persistence in keeping the dialogue going is a clear sign not only of the faith we have in God but of the faith God has in us. The process of reconciliation means a readiness on the part of each community to reach out to the other without feeling that its own political and religious identity is thereby threatened. It means accepting that compromise does not constitute surrender of principle and is not a sign of weakness, and that to make concessions does not involve the betrayal of a proud heritage. The surrender which reconciliation does involve is the surrender of intolerance, of the intolerance of difference, and the repeated pushing of difference to the point of division. It involves, rather, and above all, learning to live with difference in peace, recognizing the possibility of accommodating differences through the setting-up of structures in which those differences can coexist to the benefit of all, and each community can seek a future for itself in which the well-being of others is safeguarded.

In that age when Ireland was the envy of Europe for its culture, its learning and its sanctity, St Patrick wrote of his beloved Ireland, 'I have made you a light for the nations, so that you may be a means of salvation to the ends of the earth.' And like Paulinus here in York, of whom it was written – 'he went on straight in his calling to glorify God and edify others'. Thus, this morning in this holy place, and with the whole company of heaven, we kneel before the Father from whom every family in heaven and on earth is named; and our only prayer can be, 'Please God let there be peace.' Amen.

Five

Ecclesiastical Law Society Conference

Friday, 14 March 1997

'The letter killeth, but the spirit giveth life' (2 Corinthians 3.6)

I begin this evening with a text rather than a title, though I hope my presentation will be more in the nature of an address than a sermon. And I select this text because I believe it focuses very well and very sharply the sort of concerns which you are to address in your conference over this weekend: Practical Parish Problems: Gospel and Order. For how often have I heard this text trotted out in defence of the people getting on and doing what they want to do without reference to all those interfering lawyers who in any case cost a great deal of money! 'We are perfectly capable of ordering our own affairs, thank you very much' they say; why this dead hand of the law as it is perceived, which so often apparently stifles the inspiration and the initiative of the spirit? Well, I have to admit that in this august company I come before you to invoke those words of St Paul to the Corinthians, somewhat 'nervous and shaking with fear'. I come, too, given the subject matter of the conference, with a somewhat wry amusement, since the parish in which I began my own ministerial life and journey was one of those which in the late nineteenth century had been put under the ban, and rather revelled in it I have to say, because of its somewhat exotic ritualistic practices in a very Protestant diocese (things are very different now, thank God); two candles on the Holy table, a surpliced choir, vestments – but the most criminous thing of all: the reservation of the Sacrament. The ban lasted a number of years. However, nothing daunted, the parish in those years flourished possibly as well as it ever did, with large congregations, large numbers of vocations to the priesthood and the religious life, a vibrant parish life, and when Confirmations were needed, a flying or rather a seafaring bishop was enticed when home on furlough from one of the colonies, to do the right thing. It was of course all thoroughly illegal and one had the impression that the vicar – this particular 'reverend rebel' – together with the consider- able number of devotees which he attracted, hugely enjoyed their run-in with the diocese   for here in their view was the dead hand of the law seeking to interfere where it had no place – at the very heart of *the* charismatic event – the celebration and offering of the Holy Eucharist.

In this connection and in the process of reading myself in as Archbishop of York, I came across a somewhat robust exchange between the then Viscount Halifax (of the Malines Conversations) and Archbishop Cosmo Gordon Lang whom Halifax had understood to be considerably more sympathetic to these ritualistic practices and not least the reservation of the Sacrament, but in the process of his supporting an unfortunate incumbent who had incurred Lang's displeasure in the matter, he discovered that the archbishop was not actually wholly on his side. Such strong battles – and they were very strong indeed on these matters – are now mercifully long past, though it has to be admitted that there are occasional rumblings, stirrings even skirmishings from time to time. Nevertheless, whilst the subject matter of the confrontation may well have shifted somewhat; the possibility and the reality of confronta- tion remains, especially when it is perceived that in the translation to be found in the Revised Standard Edition of the New Testament – 'the written code kills, but the spirit gives life'.

Now it would be very tempting at this point to digress into an altogether more extended and detailed exegesis of 'law' and 'spirit' as found in Paul. The subject has attracted much writing by the commentators and in the books of New Testament theology – volume upon volume. Well, this is neither the place nor the time for such an extended digression, but I would like to make one or two more general comments, particularly when it is so often and readily read off as it were from this and other similar verses of Scripture that in Paul's mind and Paul's view 'law' and 'spirit' were implacably pitted against each other; or to put it another way, 'order' always and necessarily militates against 'Gospel'. Well, for a start, as Professor Joad always used to say on the old *Brains Trust* programme, it all depends what you mean. And indeed it does.

For my own part, I believe W. D. Davies' *Paul and Rabbinic Judaism* and Ed Sanders' *Paul and Palestinian Judaism* marked a turning-point in the Christian view of the Torah. Before their research and writing the general scenario was one in which God's people the Jews were seen to be enslaved by the law, which quenched the spirit, encouraging a merit soteriology, Pelagius-before-his-time and at his worst! Davies' and Sanders' painstaking research revealed a Torah which, far from being an enslaver, was to be seen as God's gift to the Jews for a proper and thorough ordering of the life of the people of God. He gave them manna in the wilderness to feed them, Torah to form them. Both could be perverted. Kept-over manna went sour. Torah used for the purposes of manipulation, bartering with God, or attempting to buy the favours of a God who was so priceless that he came free, deformed rather than formed. By contrast, only when Torah is seen as sheer gift (paradoxically as itself grace) it is life enhancing rather than life constricting and life distorting. Davies' and Sanders' convincing thesis is that it was precisely this 'perversion' of Torah rather than Torah itself against which Jesus and Paul raged. I note, too, in his small but telling and penetrating book on the Ten Commandments, a predecessor of mine, Archbishop Stuart Blanch, the one who in Liverpool ordained me priest, urges some caution about the straightforward use of the English word 'law' as a translation of 'Torah'; that the word 'law' itself is misleading,

'giving an impression of God as an implacable legislator handing down laws which had to be minutely observed on pain of death, seeking to restrict and inhibit us from all things we really enjoy. The original Hebrew word does not suggest that at all. It is a word meaning to teach, suggesting not a judge seated on his throne in heaven, but a father teaching his son to walk, telling him how to avoid dangers, helping him to understand himself in his relationship to and with others'

– guidelines for life and for formation – like Sanders' and Davies' Torah, itself a gift, for life.

Now, I believe that if we take such a point of view somewhat more seriously in our approach to law then an altogether more helpful, constructive and positive perspective begins to open out before us – law as gift, law itself as grace, life-giving rather than death-dealing. Furthermore, law for edification, but as well for sanctification, surely, as one of the key purposes of the Church – 'Be holy as I the Lord your God am holy.' But then there are here surely more fundamental questions about the very being and nature of the Church itself, the community of the Gospel in which law and order operate. Again, how is it possible to reconcile these two apparent opposites: law and spirit, order and Gospel. Well, I believe that if we stay with the concept of law as gift then we may begin to discover some clues as to how order and law can more harmoniously complement a community of the Gospel. There are theological and ecclesiological matters here to be addressed.

The report of the Archbishops' Commission on the organization of the Church of England, *Working as One Body*, set out in its first chapter the fundamental theological base on which the practical proposals rest. It is a theology of gracious gift –

'what underlies the way we have gone about our present task in this Commission is a theology of gracious gift; that is to say, we are convinced that God in his goodness has already given to the Church the resources it needs to be God's people, and to live and to work to his praise and glory. The most fundamental resource is that of a common fellowship or sharing in the Holy Spirit, which we enjoy as members together of the Body of Christ.'

The Commission went on further to amplify this concept of the Church as the Body of Christ, which has subsequently led some to question the almost exclusive use of this 'Body' model of the Church to the extent that it has too much dictated what in the suggested formation of an Archbishops' Council is conceived to be too much of a top down, hierarchical structure for a Church which hitherto has rather prided itself on an understanding of authority which is not substantially or wholly focused in one person, place, group or committee – even an Archbishops' Council – but which is a dispersed and distributed authority ... 'having many elements which combine, interact with, and check each other; these elements together contributing by a process of mutual support, mutual checking, and redressing of errors or exaggerations to the many sided fullness of the authority which Christ has committed to his Church' (Lambeth 1948).

Now there is here, I believe, a more fundamental question still as we look forward and look ahead to the new millennium – what kind of Church? How do we understand the meaning of this word 'Church'; for what we understand by 'Church' will surely influence the way we believe it should be structured and ordered. And here I would just like to make a comment or two on models of the Church, something the Group which I chair on behalf of the House of Bishops has been further considering and reflecting on in the light of a number of critical comments which have been received about the theological and ecclesiological basis on which the Turnbull recommendations are proposed.

As I say, the report has been criticized because it relies too much on the model of the Church as the Body of Christ – certainly a very prominent and biblical model and understanding. To be fair, however, to the authors of the report, they do go on to explicate their understanding of the Body image in a way quite contrary I would suggest to the way which it has by some come to be perceived.

Membership (of the Body) is given at baptism, and from baptism derives the radical equality of status enjoyed by all the baptised. In the Body of Christ all are sinners redeemed by grace. Within this Body the one spirit gives a variety of gifts. All these gifts are to be used in humility and love, with attentiveness to the gifts and interests of others, and with the goal of building up the whole body, and increasing its effectiveness.

And if law itself as I have suggested is a gift, a grace of God, for edification and for sanctification, how does this last sentence about humility and love – the building up of the whole body and increasing its effectiveness – how does this resonate with all of what you yourselves are involved in and with as you engage with practical parish problems? In other words, the question surely in your minds will be, given law as grace, as humility, as love, what will best serve and promote the needs of this local community as well as the wider community of the Church, not only towards the building up of the whole body and increasing its effectiveness but also and in my view more importantly towards its edification and sanctification?

There are of course other images and models of the Church in the New Testament and which I believe we also need to hold before us and to keep before us in this whole endeavour. For these serve us well in that balancing and checking function of which the Lambeth Conference so well and effectively speaks. There is, for example, the model of the Church as servant, as herald, as pilgrim, as communion. And if you focus in a very particular and exclusive way on one particular model, for example the Church as pilgrim – a Church on the move, a Church on the way, a Church travelling light – and then go on to ask in the light of such an understanding therefore what kind of structures, what kind of order and law are required, you will I suspect get very short shrift. And you know as well as I that there are such individuals, groups, parishes, organizations, both within and without the Church of England which do have a particular view – this or some other – which seeks to abandon and jettison the accumulated baggage of the past which not only bears down upon us but weighs us down so that it becomes impossible to move on and forge ahead when it is believed the Holy Spirit is so leading us.

Like Avery Dulles, in his book *Models of the Church*, I should want to argue that it is neither biblical nor realistic to pursue so limited and exclusive an ecclesiology. Indeed in any view such a pursuit leads only to schism, even heresy, in that in all heresy there is the going over the top, as it were, the going to seed of what basically is a valid and valued insight, but when pressed so relentlessly and exclusively becomes not only a hindrance but a positive stumbling-block. Dulles writes:

> Our method must be to harmonize the models in such a way that their differences become complementary rather than mutually repugnant ... we must refrain from so affirming any one of the models as to deny, even implicitly, what the others affirm. In this way it may be possible to gain an understanding of the Church that transcends the limitations of any given model.

And he concludes

> The future forms of the Church lie beyond our power to foresee, except that we may be sure that they will be different from the forms of yesterday and today. The Church will not necessarily mirror the secular society of tomorrow, for it must avoid the kind of conformity with the world condemned by Paul in Romans 12.2. On the other hand the Church will have to make adjustments in order to survive in the society of the future and to confront the members of that society with the challenge of the Gospel.'

And this is precisely, surely, what *Working as One Body* is itself about.

Thus in response to the question I posed a little time ago now – what kind of Church shall we need to ensure that that balance, the interplay, the checks and balances, the suppleness and elasticity which have been characteristic of our Church since its beginnings and which remain necessary if we are truly to discern some sense of direction for the future, my response would be that we need also some sense of connectedness and continuity, as Charles Handy puts it. What then of 'law'? What are we to say? I have suggested that if we are to endorse and embrace the basic theological assertion of *Working as One Body*, which I believe we should and must, the theology of gracious gift, then this needs to permeate every aspect of our life as 'Church'. This is the context, surely, in which we pursue our witness, our ministry and our mission.

And as members of the Ecclesiastical Law Society you

yourselves will, I take it, be open to these same theological and ecclesiological insights as establishing some basic general principles for the practicalities of your work, and even where you are dealing with faculty applications for a memorial tablet in the church, for the removal of bodies or remains from a burial ground, holding a court in some hotly disputed matter or because you are formally and legally caught up in one of those indeterminable and intractable breakdowns of pastoral relationships, in all these practicalities which can so often become a 'scandal' – and I use the word both in its New Testament as well as in its tabloid sense – you will not lose sight of these altogether more positive and grace-given principles. Do they offer any better way forward in assisting parties in disute towards reconciliation, even though a decision may have gone against one of the parties? What of the tyranny of the majority, if I may so describe it, for that is how it can often appear to the losers?

How far does your decision, your judgement serve towards the building up of the Church and its effectiveness, its edification and sanctification? The law itself can and should operate as gift and as grace in a Church which celebrates its life as a gracious gift of God.

Now it seems to me that Archbishop Geoffrey Fisher's expressed view about the function of canon law quoted by Mark Hill in volume 4 of the *Ecclesiastical Law Journal* that 'the dominant note of canon law is not one of legal restriction or of enforcement by charge and punishment. The general purpose of the Canons is to set out a generally agreed norm or standard of behaviour to govern the family affairs of the Church' – that this statement chimes well with a view of law/ order as a 'charism' in the Church which has as a basic ecclesiological principle the theology of gracious gift. Moreover, I would suggest that in that well-expressed view of authority deriving from Lambeth 48, law/order itself is one of those elements which properly provide the checks and balances of the Church. It does not and cannot operate entirely on its own or within the confines of its own domain, but rather as one of the many elements, distributed and dispersed, throughout the Church. I am also reminded of the opening sentence of the Preface of the Book of Common Prayer which expresses well the purpose of the law and with which Archbishop Fisher's statement resonates almost exactly:

> It hath been the wisdom of the Church of England, ever since the first compiling of her public liturgy to keep the mean between the two extremes, of too much stiffness in refusing and of too much easiness in admitting any variation from it.

And there will be many instances in which I suspect you could all well recall that your basic purpose has been precisely that – the keeping of the mean between two extremes. And if such a 'mean' is to be kept then I believe there does need to be flexibility; that where such matters are concerned we shall, perhaps in the shaping and forming of legislation, be the less anxious about dotting every 'i' and crossing every 't' lest in so doing we load upon our successors burdens impossible for them to bear.

Here I am reminded of one of the archdeacons – and he was by no means the only one – who at a recent gathering of archdeacons at High Leigh raised a question about the Pastoral Measure and its operation. Given the current situation in almost every diocese throughout the Church of England, where strategies are being fashioned and formed bearing in mind the limited numbers of stipendiary clergy available over the next five years or so, the question was asked, Does not that which was once heralded as a great deliverance in its day, the Pastoral Measure, become in changed times and circumstances and if applied according to the exact and literal letter, a burden which binds rather than liberates?

Again, if I may speak on a matter in which I was involved more personally in the Diocese of London, the shaping and creating of what came to be called the London Plan in the wake of the Ordination of Women as Priests Measure and which in its turn influenced considerably the provisions presently obtaining under the Act of Synod. I am well aware that there was no precedent for any such arrangement, and on my first putting somewhat tentatively what was in my mind to a number of legal advisers, the response was plainly that it could not be done. The clear response to almost every proposal, every question, was 'no'. However, being one of those quietly determined sorts of persons, I pursued the matter further, not simply on a fudge it/fix it kind of basis, but rather on precisely the principles which I have been setting out in this paper – that is, for the building up of the Church, for its edification and sanctification, given that there were clear and persisting strong divergent and differing views on the subject of the ordination of women even given the Synod vote – how is it possible for us to live in the highest possible degree of communion and what arrangements would be thus in the Church's best interests? Now, I could speak at much greater length and in considerably greater detail. I should not wish to be wanting to claim too much for such arrangements as we now have in place which I entirely admit are themselves anomalous – but no more or less anomalous, I would suggest, than the actual provisions in the Measure which, if they had been operated as envisaged, would undoubtedly have led to 'no go' dioceses and done substantially greater damage to the Church of England in the immediate as well as in the longer term. The point I want to emphasize is that neither the London Plan nor the Act of Synod set out detailed provisions. They offered a framework, some broad principles, that 'mean' between the two extremes of which the Preface to the Book of Common Prayer speaks, the *regula*, not the detailed rules to govern the family affairs of the Church, in which and with which the Church seeks to live through this disputed question, mindful of the urgency of the mission entrusted to it by the Saviour to go into all the world and preach the Gospel. More importantly, given the world itself wounded, torn, divided and rent asunder in all manner of ways, the overwhelming question at all times in my mind was how was it possible for the Church, quite properly preaching its message of reconciliation, renewal and hope, how was it possible given the division within its own ranks to reflect these very ingredients in the shaping and fashioning of its own continuing life?

I rather suspect I may have begun to go somewhat beyond my brief for this evening. Nevertheless, I hope that I have been able to set before you some more general thoughts and reflections, setting out as it were the backdrop to the more detailed and practical matters with which you will be further occupied during the course of this conference.

Six

Installation of new Superior – Community of the Resurrection, Mirfield

Feast of the Epiphany, 6 January 1998

'When they saw the star, they rejoiced exceedingly with great joy' (Matthew 2.10)

Among the presents I received at Christmas – socks, handkerchiefs, shirt and tie, a couple of bottles of scotch – always necessary for survival – there were as well two books in particular: *Furious Interiors* and *Not Bosses but Leaders*. I did just wonder whether someone was trying to tell me something about myself! The first of course is the recent paperback version of the life of R. S. Thomas; the second a now fairly old book by John Adair, one-time Professor of Leadership Studies in the University of Surrey. And as I read again the account of the journey of the Magi, in these days when leadership skills, leadership studies, strategic management and so on are all the rage, I did just begin to wonder how the Magi had made it, without the assistance of our modern wisdom in these matters.

Now whilst it happens to be quite fortuitous, it is nevertheless very appropriate that the installation of your new Superior, Crispin, is taking place on this feast day of the Epiphany of our Lord. And may I just add what a particular and personal pleasure it is for me that it happens to have fallen to me to have been entrusted with this duty, for it is some forty or so years now that I have known Crispin, both of us, two of many who, I suspect, owe their vocation to Plumi, the feared yet much-loved and respected Chaplain of those days of St Peter's Convent. I will not elaborate more now on the many stories that could be told! The John Adair book to which I have referred is enormously quotable. I will not bore you further this morning, but I would nevertheless just like to set before you one sentence which struck me personally quite forcibly, especially in these days when people seem to be clamouring endlessly for leadership and for speaking out – and of course when they get it they resent it and reject it. 'A leader is best when people barely know that he or she exists.' And that is the challenge I believe which is before you, Crispin, as we install you in your office as Superior of this Community of the Resurrection. And as we do so, what is there, I ask myself, in the Matthean narrative of the Magi which might be of some assistance to us? Already I have mentioned, somewhat facetiously perhaps, that there is not much about leadership when it comes to the three Wise Men. And why not? The answer must surely be that they simply had no need of it, because already they had a vision – 'We have seen his star in the East and are come to worship him.' Each of them so captivated by this bright and shining star that there could be no question either of the direction or of the goal of their journey – the child in the manger.

So what of the journey and the goal so far as this Community is concerned, recognizing that your new Superior's term of office will lead you well into the new millennium? I would suggest that perhaps there are some clues for us in those gifts which the Wise Men bore to the Infant Christ and which are both the vision and the gift of the Community as you yourselves journey on; three signs to which you are to be attentive in your life together in Christ.

Frankincense is a reminder of what is at the heart of it all: the praise and worship of God. 'Lift up your heart to God in humble love and mean God himself and not what you get out of him ...' writes the author of the *Cloud of Unknowing*. We can, if we are not careful, become so attentive to the directing and advising in the matter of things spiritual to and for others that we ourselves become castaways; we need to guard our own space and that of the Community not for the pursuit of our own religiosity, but to ensure that rather than becoming overwhelmed by the multifarious demands continuing to be made upon you, you might rather give yourselves the opportunity of being the more overwhelmed by God.

The gift of gold speaks to us of the gift of the kingdom: God's kingdom of righteousness and truth and justice, the good tidings which Jesus brings to the poor, the proclaiming of release to captives, the recovery of sight to the blind, the setting at liberty those who are oppressed. This is the good tidings which you are to bring to the world today. Here is the very crucible in which as a Community you were forged: a community of hope – a community of incarnation – a community of atonement – all of these titles rejected by Gore in favour of the then Society of the Resurrection; Gore, of whom Alan Wilkinson comments 'opened men's eyes to the glory of God and the needs of the poor' in words reminiscent of John Chrysostom's: 'God has no need of golden temples, but of golden hearts.' There are questions here for the whole Church as well as for yourselves as together we seek to engage altogether more radically the spiritual and the social, both of which are the focus of our vocation in the world.

What finally are we to make of the myrrh – the myrrh of suffering and of entombment? Perhaps there is a connection here with that somewhat enigmatic and paradoxical sentence about leadership – 'a leader is best when people barely know that he exists'. Such a statement is a contradiction and a protest against much of what is both written and expected in terms of leadership today. And from those very earliest monastic communities in the Egyptian desert, protest and contradiction have been potent signs of the monastic movement. We need no flight into any desert today, for as T. S. Eliot reminds us

The desert is not remote in southern tropics,
The desert is not only around the corner,
The desert is squeezed in the tube train next to you,
The desert is in the heart of your brother.

– and in so many hearts and lives today.

So how are the particular signs of protest and contradiction, the call to poverty, chastity and obedience, truly liberating individuals and the Community as a whole to live Christ's risen life – to bring life to others; to give light to the world – among the people and in the very places we are set – starting with ourselves and each other? I would not presume to give you answers, but I do urge you all this day – a day of exceeding great joy for us all as Crispin is installed as Superior – that each one of you use the opportunity to present afresh and anew before the infant Saviour and each other those gifts of frankincense and gold and myrrh; yes the fed-upness with each other and the grumpiness and the grumbling, as well as the sheer thankfulness for God's mercy and God's grace in calling you here and in the gift which He makes to you of each other.

And by the way, do not either forget Silvanus – a very faithful brother – who has seen the Community through some pretty trying and testing times and circumstances. Make sure he has now some respite and refreshment. Perhaps his best gift from the Community might be what I often recommend to clergy taking sabbaticals and who come up with all sorts of intense suggestions for study and the writing-up of reports or experiences, when you know perfectly well what they really need is a jolly good holiday – give him a bucket and spade and send him on his way rejoicing!

Seven

University of Leeds – Chaplaincy Sermon

Wednesday, 4 February 1998 – For the healing of the nations

'Is not this the fast I choose ... to break every yoke'? (Isaiah 58.6)

It is just over one hundred and forty years ago now, a hundred and forty years and two months to be precise, that the intrepid explorer David Livingstone delivered an address in the Senate House at Cambridge on 4 December 1857 which was to have a transformative effect on Christianity both here at home and overseas; here, the formation of a missionary society, though now with a different name and still very much in business today especially in Africa; overseas, the opening up of numerous lands to the Christian mission. During the course of his lecture Livingstone shared with them in some detail his own experiences in Africa where he had first gone in 1840. The slave trade was rife and vicious and he felt passionately about its wickedness. Towards the end of his speech the point of it all became very clear indeed: 'My desire is to open a path to this district, that civilisation, commerce and Christianity might find their way there ... The natives of Central Africa are very desirous of trading, but their only traffic is at present in slaves, of which the poorer people have an unmitigated horror; it is therefore most desirable to encourage the former principle, and thus open a way for the consumption of free productions, and the introduction of Christianity and commerce.' And so in the very same vein he concluded, 'I beg to direct your attention to Africa ... I go back to Africa to try to make an open path for commerce and Christianity; do you carry out the work which I have begun.' That was Livingstone's call and summons. And it was a second wrangler graduate in the mathematical tripos of the same University of Cambridge, Charles Frederick Mackenzie, subsequently ordained priest and who became an archdeacon, who was consecrated in Cape Town at the formal request of the Church of England as 'Bishop of the Mission to the tribes dwelling in the neighbourhood of the Lake Nyasa and River Shire.' It was indeed a novel idea and the title has everything of the ring of the primitive Church about it. And what a portrait of episcopal ministry as Mackenzie remarks in his diary! 'I myself have in my left hand a loaded gun, in my right the crosier they gave me in Cape Town, in front a can of oil and behind a bag of seeds, which I carry the greater part of the day. I thought of the contrast between my weapon and my staff, the one like Jacob, the other like Abraham, who armed his trained servants to rescue Lot. I thought of the seed which we must sow in the hearts of the people, and of the oil of the spirit that must strengthen us in all we do.' As one historian commented, 'And so at length in Africa the sower went forth to sow his seed.' Inevitably, given the time and given the circumstances, it was a mission which was perilous in the extreme, fraught with enormous difficulty and ridden with disease, a mission which sent men to their deaths, a mission which ultimately had to be withdrawn. Yet out of failure, the seed of new beginnings of work already established in Zanzibar by Bishop Mackenzie and subsequently gradually spreading eastward, was to be the harbinger not only of the abolition of the slave trade in those parts, but of a flourishing, thriving and growing life both of Christianity and of commerce in Africa.

The three words which featured so prominently in Livingstone's speech were: Christianity, commerce, civilization. For he fervently believed that the three were so closely interrelated that civilization could only follow Christianity and commerce. Here were riches for the taking, riches in terms of a people presently in the dark night of heathen ignorance, to be brought into the marvellous light of Christ; riches in terms of a land to be opened up and where international trade and commerce could only yield great rewards for the people; and the two in turn would inevitably usher in the dawn of a new civilization for the present, and great hope for the future for the people of these parts. Indeed Livingstone went so far as to describe both Christianity and commerce as 'the two pioneers of civilisation'. Now in the context of the theme of this evening's sermon – For the healing of the nations – a consideration of the nature of mission for the millennium, these three words used by Livingstone provide us, I believe, with a very appropriate framework on which to base our reflections. So what then today are we to make of these three: Christianity, commerce, civilisation?

In the first place the call had been for men – that this nation, this country in particular, should provide as missionaries 'men of education, standing, enterprise, zeal and piety'. There are those who have since that time questioned the whole notion of the sending of missionaries in quite the same way as Livingstone had called. And yet missionaries have followed in huge numbers and still do, and still, I believe, should. The whole basis of their going may have changed very considerably; the theological understanding of mission has perhaps enabled us to see the world-wide mission of the Church much more as partnership than philanthropy. But however it may have been understood or interpreted there can be no doubt of the huge contribution made by those who have gone forth from these islands believing that their vocation has been one of total self-giving, self-dedication, yes, often heroic self-sacrifice to the cause of Christ in foreign lands. And that is still a noble vocation, so that that fullness of life which Christ wills for all might be achieved in all and for all.

I had recently the great privilege of attending on behalf of the Archbishop of Canterbury at the end of September this year the Golden Jubilee Celebrations of the Church of South India. There in the compound of St George's Cathedral, Madras, in the torrid humidity of that huge and sprawling city, some fifteen thousand or so people from all over southern India had gathered. One of the many highlights for me – and there were quite a number during what seemed to be an almost continuous three-day celebration – was the calling onto the platform and the presentation of the 'missionaries'; those who fifty, even sixty or so years ago had gone out and gone forth from this land often in the face of huge obstacles and without the assistance of modern medical prophylactics of any kind. They were all women – a marked contrast to Livingstone's call for 'men'. These women had taught the Christian faith, they had given those of all faiths or of none a basic education – to read and to write. They had gone out as nurses and doctors, establishing centres of health care and medicine, and their testimony remains in the cities and the villages of southern India. In speaking to this huge assembly at one of the main gatherings of the celebration the Speaker of the Indian Parliament, himself a Christian, paid tribute to the contribution which these Christian women had made to education in India, an education free and available for any who wanted it. I was taken to the Christian Medical College in Vellore, now a large and impressive eighteen-hundred-bed medical centre dealing with every specialism you might find in a similar centre in this country. This centre itself is the result of a one-bed clinic planted as a seed by an American missionary, Ida Scudder, some ninety-seven years ago now. She saw her work from the very beginning as a calling and a challenge by God and devoted herself wholly to the health needs of the people of India, particularly women and children. And I saw also how the work and influence of that centre has spread out and developed into a very considerable community health and development programme. Here is a holistic approach such as I witnessed in a number of similar initiatives during a visit to Tanzania some twelve years ago now, which is dedicated to the overall well-being of both the individual and the community. The activities of such a programme combine health care, education, social and economic development. The comprehensive character of these programmes is well described in one of their booklets – 'Community health and development is not only confined to healing or income generating activities but also places high priority to make people aware of their rights and responsibilities and self-sufficiency.'

There can be little doubt that in such initiatives established in the past and sustained into the present and for the future there is the clear fulfilment of the Isaianic vision of God's kingdom, the loosing of the yoke of ignorance and disease, the light of education, healing and health care breaking forth like the dawn.

However, it is by no means a one-way traffic. One of the exciting things about the way partnerships have developed between Churches, dioceses, parishes, deaneries is the mutuality of exchange, the recognition that there are gifts and skills, insights and values which each have for the benefit of the other. The arrival of missionaries on these shores is a welcome sign that together we share in mission, which is God's call and God's challenge to us all wherever and whoever we may be. To find, therefore, a missionary from Tanzania living and working on a housing estate in West Yorkshire ought not to come as any surprise, and there is much that we need to learn from our brothers and sisters in Christ from other lands. How fresh and vital, exciting and expectant their Christian faith is, so often a striking contrast to its tired, drab and dreary Western counterpart. So there is some sense in which we can look with a degree of satisfaction – a degree of satisfaction which I think Livingstone might have approved – at the history of the Christian mission to Africa: a history which, having gone full circle, now demonstrates the proper mutuality and interdependence of the whole missionary process.

But the second significant word in Livingstone's speech was 'commerce'. In the exploration which he had already made in that part of Africa he had both witnessed and discovered great potential. He spoke about it with enthusiasm:

> In a commercial point of view, communication with this country is desirable. Angola is wonderfully fertile, produ-cing every kind of tropical plant in rank luxuriance. Passing on to the valley of Kwango the stalk of the grass was as thick as a quill and towered above my head, although I was mounted on my ox; cotton is produced in great abundance ... bananas and pineapples grow in great luxuriance ... the country on the other side is not quite so fertile, but, in addition to indigo, cotton and sugar cane, produces a fibrous substance which I am assured is stronger than flax.

And he saw not only a 'land flowing with milk and honey', he saw, too, a people with a real flair for trading. And although that flair was then largely in the slave business, he foresaw that by 'encouraging the native propensity for trade, the advantages that might be derived in a commercial point of view are incalculable'.

So, what of this trade and commerce? Has its success matched that of the Church's missionary endeavour? And has our involvement with it been attended by the same selfless giving and dedication? In his vivid description Livingstone made mention, amongst other things, of bananas, growing in great abundance. Whilst bananas may not be one of the major exports of that part of Africa they nevertheless figure considerably in this nation's diet. We eat 14 million of them every day and they are close to overtaking apples as the nation's most popular fruit. In 1995, for example, the UK imported 515 million kilos of bananas worth £300 million. Sixty-five percent of these came from the Caribbean region. One supermarket alone sells eight million bananas a week, more than any other single item. All this may be good news for us on our side of the trade equation, but what about those on the other side? What of the terms and conditions for those in the Caribbean, most of them working small family farms on hilly islands with high production costs, who, because of these costs, cannot compete with the large plantations of central America: Large plantations where labour costs are driven down by harsh and repressive means? And if bananas are 'big' in our national diet, then coffee, at an average of 3.06 cups per person per day, is equally 'big' in the nation's drinking. Sales of coffee exceed £80 million a year and, interestingly enough, nearly 90 per cent is in the form of instant coffee. Again, and periodic 'blips' in the shelf price apart, it is good news for us; but what about those on the other side of the equation? Take, for example, those who actually harvest the coffee. For them life can only be described as precarious. The harvest lasts for three to four months of the year and then they are out of work. Wages for the Brazilian pickers average out at something like £73 per month, but bills for rent and utilities eat up around £60 of that. So, faced with impossible arithmetic such as this, it is small wonder that workers see taking their small children out of school and setting them to work in the plantation as the only way to survive. There is, of course, far more to this question of trade than bananas and coffee – already you will recognize the huge questions concerning the commercial aspects of their production, export and consumption. Trade in food will always remain for many third world countries, a major, if not *the* major, plank in their national economies. What Livingstone had to say about the rich fertility of the land is in large part as true now as it was then. The people, too, remain every bit as bound up in the cultivation of those lands. So that the export of foodstuffs is inevitably and quite properly an important, if not the only, source of income and employment for many millions in the third world. An important and *increasing* source of income. So how does the way in which all this has developed square with Livingstone's vision for the future – Christianity, commerce, civilization? The increase in third world agricultural trading may be truly impressive, but it has also come at huge cost to many agricultural workers. And alongside the people we should not forget the land, for the land also suffers. We are all well aware of the dangers of large-scale land clearance and drainage. But producing food for the global markets has another downside. It requires the use of highly intensive growing methods; massive use of chemical fertilizers and pesticides; heavy irrigation – all of which inevitably have a cumulatively damaging effect on the land. All in all, the picture of how Livingstone's second great principle, commerce, is shaping up in the late twentieth century can only be described as 'gloomy'. There is just too much of a sense in which commerce has come to be synonymous with exploitation: an exploitation which, in its grosser manifestations, fatally compromises the path toward civilization. And all too often we have seen evidence of the viciously destructive power of the cocktail of exploitation and poverty, not to mention the huge and crippling debt with which so many of the Third World nations are burdened today. There can be little doubt as to where the weight of responsibility for this debt lies. It lies firmly at the door of the Western world. And thirty years of lending – lending which can most charitably be described as 'inappropriate' – and I am very well aware of the corrupt leaders and the corrupt regimes to which we were quite content to continue lending – this has now reached a point where the cumulative weight of debt has pushed the already poor into a grinding poverty. Lending, which was euphemistically termed as 'aid', has effectively *bankrupted* many of the receiving countries. But use of the term *bankrupted* is not welcomed in international monetary circles. Governments, it is protested, cannot by definition or by law be declared bankrupt. Therefore, the debt must stand. But wait: in our 'civilized' West the mechanism by which individual bankrupts are discharged from their debt is well recognized and accepted. It draws a line. It enables people to pick up the pieces and begin life over again. It is a humane device and part of the mechanism of a caring and civilized *society*. And it ought properly to have a place in dealings between nations in a civilized *world*. Such a notion is far from new. Two hundred years ago, Adam Smith called for 'fair, open and avowed' proceedings in dealing with the debts of states – dealings which he was at pains to liken to dealing with the debts of individuals. That is to say, matters should be conducted in a way that is 'least dishonourable to the debtor and least hurtful to the creditor'.

So how is it possible even to begin to consider and propose an altogether more positive and creative way forward? It seems that hardly a dozen words are strung together these days without some mention being made of the millennium. There is, however, *one* millennial gesture which could set our world ablaze with real hope. Launched in 1996 by Britain's three major aid agencies and supported by all the mainstream Christian Churches, the Jewish Reformed Synagogue and many other organizations, it is known as *Jubilee 2000*. It is a call to start the new millennium by giving a new and debt-free start to over a billion people. As Livingstone was speaking, the curse of human slavery had still not been entirely eliminated from the world's economic order. But within a few years it had been effectively rooted out. If so great a step was possible then, it should be every bit as possible *now* to root out today's slavery – the curse of third world debt. And *that* is the summons and the challenge of *Jubilee 2000*.

Christianity, commerce ... and on to civilization. But is it my imagination or do we these days hear rather *less* about civilization and rather *more* about globalization? Are there not more golden opportunities in the global market place for us who live in the global village? And are there not ever fewer barriers to the movement of capital and goods? And fewer barriers still to the flow of information and technology? And as all these barriers come down, so the opportunities open up. Or do they? Or more precisely perhaps, for *whom* do they open up? If the global market *can* be described as a 'level playing field' then it is evidently more level for some than it is for others. It is, to put it bluntly, a playing field *only* for those with the economic muscle to get up there, and *stay* there. For the strong get stronger and the weak get weaker – and globalization proves *not* to be providing a home or a market place for everyone. Too many are squeezed out; too many are left powerless. I think that, with Livingstone, I prefer the other '-isation': civilization. There is a loftiness of spirit about civilization to which the relentlessness of globalization can never aspire. While civilization leads and encourages, globalization forces a remorseless, unyielding pace. While civilization builds up, globalization too often drives down. Civilization is altogether gentler and more enabling and empowering – seeking to share; seeking to give. And perhaps most telling of all, civilization is about *people*, their aspirations and their potential. In contrast, all that marks globalization are the inexorable processes of expansion. I believe that it is to engage with the growth and development of civilization that we in the West are called. And we – that is our governments, our financial institutions, our commercial enterprises *and we ourselves* – will only do so to the extent that we commit ourselves to dealing with our brothers and sisters in the third world with equity *and with generosity*. It was Gladstone who said that 'the resources of civilisation are not yet exhausted'. But what about today? Well, it all depends. If, as the millennium draws to its close, the Western world can bring itself to exhibit in its actions something of its Christian heritage and the Christian moral tradition, a new asceticism, then Gladstone's words may still hold good. And in this context, it is important to recognize that we in the West are *not* being called to some sort of dreary sacrifice. As Livingstone protested, when some spoke to him of the 'sacrifice' he had made by spending himself in Africa, responding with a typical alacrity and forthrightness:

Can that be called a sacrifice which is simply paid back as a small part of a great debt owing to our God, which we can never repay? Sacrifice? Away with the word, in such a view, and with such a thought! It is emphatically no sacrifice. Say, rather, it is a privilege.

For us today, it is neither privilege nor sacrifice: rather the privilege of sacrifice.

Eight

St Matthew's, Carver Street, Sheffield

Monday, 29 June 1998

'The bread which I shall give for the life of the world is my flesh' (John 6.51)

One of the many features of my home at Bishopthorpe is the considerable number of portraits of my predecessors. From the time of entering to the time of leaving there they all are, looking out, looking down – not on the whole a very cheerful group – and William Thomson (of whom it was once said that he would never really be very happy in heaven because he was far too interested in being militant on earth) is no exception. His look this evening was distinctly chilly! He was the first and the last archbishop to come here.

The controversy which raged a hundred years ago puts the controversies of today into the shade! The vituperative comments which passed between parish priest and archbishop provided the *Sheffield Daily Telegraph* with page after page of copy as both of them, increasingly antagonized by and frustrated with each other, resorted to publishing openly their correspondence. But the war of words in the press was more than matched by the war in the pews: demonstrations, skirmishings and brawlings in the church itself, in which the unrelentingly Protestant churchwarden, Walter Wynn, having caused three people to be ejected from a certain pew, was himself struck on the head by a lady's umbrella resulting in a cracked skull. The legal proceedings which he subsequently initiated went against him – he retreated from the fray, directing henceforth all his energies to a rival Protestant 'St Matthew's' Mission. We may well look back now with a somewhat wry amusement on such events. But they were real, and passionate and hard-fought, because on both sides there was at the heart of it all a driving conviction and concern about the truth of the Gospel. And not unlike those controversies of the early centuries concerning the nature and the person of Jesus Christ, this particular controversy rumbled and raged on for many subsequent years.

So what was all the fuss about? Why such disputes, controversies, divisions? As already I have hinted it was because the various contenders believed that what was at stake was the very truth of the Gospel itself – the truth about Jesus Christ and the implications of that greatest and most mysterious truth of all, that in that child born in a manger there was the creator of the universe. No wonder so many writers and commentators can in the end only resort to the phrase *magnum mysterium*. Here in this eucharistic celebration we are in the presence of that same *magnum mysterium*. For that is what the Church of the ages, of which this Church of England claims to be a part – the One, Holy, Catholic and Apostolic Church – has unfailingly believed, so that in the Book of Common Prayer we pray that we may so 'eat the flesh of thy dear Son Jesus Christ, and drink his blood, that our sinful bodies may be made clean by his body and our souls washed through his most precious blood and that we may evermore dwell in him, and he in us.' The whole purpose of the reservation of the sacrament, begun 100 years ago to this day, is both to celebrate and to honour that basic and fundamental truth of our faith: 'And the Word became flesh and dwelt among us ... and we beheld his glory.' And that same glory we continue to behold, as in the 'real presence' of the Lord we fall to our knees; we pause and we pray in adoration, in wonder, love and praise. Such can be the only response of frail humanity in the sacramental presence of the living and loving God.

At the heart of the Catholic revival there was the centrality of the Eucharist with the desire for the worshipping of God in the beauty of holiness. Those struggles about the wearing of vestments, the use of candles on the Holy Table, the reservation of the Sacrament, were never intended to become struggles simply about the sanctuary and its ornamentation. Rather, these were the very means, the outward and visible signs and symbols of the inwardness of these holy and awesome mysteries which would lead the worshipper more deeply and more fully into the practice of the presence of Christ – at all times, in all places – Christ dwelling in us and we in Him. Furthermore, the sacrificial aspect of this Eucharist was reflected in sacrificial living: a simplicity of life, a rule of life, lives lived out of love for God and others.

We need urgently, I believe, to recover that perseverance in prayer out of which sprang much which was so attractive and compelling. There is the need for a new asceticism, for a more definite commitment to that *cantus firmus* of daily prayer, where we shall undoubtedly from time to time be inconvenienced; not trying to fit our Christian discipleship around everything else which increasingly crowds in upon us and claims our time, but where the clear priorities in terms of perseverance in prayer – prayer daily, our presence at the Holy Eucharist, the sacrament of penance and reconciliation, that deep reflective reading of Holy Scripture – all that which in short is the very stuff of Christian living, that which is described as 'holiness of life', actually make this a prime concern – a life or death matter, because that is precisely what it is. And it is no use sharing or enabling or affirming it, we actually need to get down on our knees and do something about it. In brief, in the words of the New Testament, 'watch and pray'.

Notice that it is 'for the life of the world' that this bread of life is given. The mission entrusted by Christ to His Church does not begin and end here, nor can it only be confined to the four walls of this or any church. We are sent out and sent forth. Here was one of the greatest strengths of the Catholic movement in the Church of England, one of its greatest converting attractions – that clergy and laity were together keenly involved in the work of evangelization and service.

It is from our participation in this Holy Sacrifice that we are sent, ourselves, our souls and bodies, to be a living sacrifice of love and service in God's world. There was about the movement at its zenith a real energy for evangelization – that indefatigable and indomitable zeal for the winning of souls for Christ. And it was not simply the great priestly names – the Mackonochies, the Stantons and the Ommanneys – the 'Reverend Rebels' – of the Catholic revival either; it was as much the contribution of the laity which drew many ordinary women and men to a love for the Lord Jesus Christ and a deeper care and compassion for each other. The energy for evangelization, for that going out and loving and serving the Lord in the world, particularly among the poor and the needy, the lonely and the unloved, the old just as much as the young, is the responsibility of each and every one of us. The initiatives in evangelization inspired a comprehensive programme of social action, not least in the most depressed and most squalid parts of our large industrial towns, areas which otherwise the Church of England simply would not and could not have touched. But here was no 'social gospel'; rather here was yet another demonstration of the truth of the Incarnation and our understanding of God's creative activity; the right of every human person to that dignity, respect and recognition of one who is created in the image and likeness of God. It is a truth which is at the heart of the Gospel. Alliances were made and partnerships forged with others in the community, civic and voluntary, long before *Faith in the City* and the Church Urban Fund. And this social action again reflects the continuity and connectedness with the Church down the ages. It was St John Chrysostom in the fourth century who challenged the Christian community – a challenge relevant in and for every age – 'Remember that he who said "This is my body", and made good his words, also said "You saw me hungry and you gave me no food, and in so far as you did it not to one of these, you did it not to me"' Adorn your churches if you will, but do not forget your brothers and sisters in distress … God has no need of golden vessels, but of golden hearts.

So this night as we celebrate one hundred years of the reservation of the Blessed Sacrament in this church – of that bread given for the life of the world – a continuing outward and visible sign, a sacramental sign of God with us and alongside us for ever, we give thanks and praise to Him who is the Lord of all things. Lord of our lives, Lord of His Church, Lord of all creation. We join our voices with those of angels and archangels, with Peter and Paul, with Blessed Mary and the whole company of heaven, as in our prayer and praise on earth, in the offering of these holy and sacred mysteries, we ourselves are caught up in wonder, love and praise – a glimpse of God's glory here on earth – a sign of that future to which we are all called, God's gift of faith and hope and love for you and for me and for the peoples of the whole world; for 'the bread which I shall give for the life of the world is my flesh ... whoever eats of this bread will live for ever ... Lord evermore give us this bread.'

Nine

Order of the Holy Paraclete, Whitby – Profession of Sister Pam

Thursday, 17 September 1998

'In this is love, not that we loved God but that he loved us' (1 John 4.10)

One of the most heartening and encouraging aspects of the recent Lambeth Conference at Canterbury was the sight of representatives of the religious communities of the Church of England among us for some twenty-four hours at the invitation of the Archbishop of Canterbury. It came as a considerable surprise to quite a large number of bishops that there were monks and nuns at all in the Anglican Communion. It was even more of a surprise to quite a number of our own bishops that there were so many, younger as well as older, and these but representatives of a considerably larger number. The whole Conference was already much in debt to those members of religious communities who had agreed to ensure and serve the daily liturgical events – and it was certainly hard work, I observed, trying to ensure that the wishes and desires of the respective Churches were met in terms of worship. Above all, though, it was the silent space at the centre of the whole campus – a modest octagonal building in which throughout the whole Conference from beginning to end there was a prayerful presence – the utter silence of the place a welcome relief from the cacophony outside; it was here I believe where the religious orders made their greatest contribution. We needed the religious orders more than we could say as they bore in and through their prayer the spiritual struggles with which such a conference inevitably engages.

Today we rejoice that another member, Sister Pam, is being added to that great company of those like yourselves who have made their life profession.

Today I would suggest, is in the first place a celebration of God's graciousness and God's goodness – certainly towards you, Pam, but also in and through you for the rest of us too. For it is to this place and this moment that your life journey and your life story is now gathered and focused, caught up as it is, as we all are, in this eucharistic celebration, into the movement of Christ's own self-offering to the Father. Your story is special, it is particular, it is unique. Above all it is the story of the God who has brought you through all the changing scenes of life, whose presence and power has been at work in and with you and around you when probably you yourself have least understood or experienced it so to be. And so it is with us all, quite irrespective of whether we are members of this community or not. For what today does is to set before us in this final profession the ultimate challenge of the profession of Christian faith and life – the challenge of Christian conversion. For Pam this growth into that primordial baptismal sacrament, into the death and resurrection of Jesus Christ, has brought her to this day, this place and this community. And the challenge to us all – to the whole Church which the monastic movement sets before us is that radical call of Jesus Christ to forsake all and follow Him.

There have been, of course, those who have heard that call of the Gospel and responded, we may conclude, in somewhat extraordinary, extravagant, even crazy ways. Yet how else is it possible to respond to that crazy and profligate love of God which first loved us and goes on loving us endlessly, eternally, even when we are most undeserving, when we ourselves have strayed far from that love, even placed ourselves, as we may consider it, quite outside and beyond its reach? The sheer wonder of it is, of course, that here in God's love is an upholding and an enfolding from which nothing at all, even our worst selves, can separate us – 'nor height, nor depth, or things present, or things to come – nor life, nor death – nor anything else in all creation will be able to separate us from the love of God in Christ Jesus our Lord'. Yet here is no 'love God and do as you like' kind of prescription. Rather because God so loved us and goes on loving us, our only response can be to seek to reciprocate that love: love the Lord your God, with all your heart, with all your soul, with all your mind, with all your strength – and your neighbour as yourself. That's the sting in the tail. For the challenge and the struggle for us of this profligacy of God is our own mean-mindedness and self-centredness with my neighbour and with myself.

The profession which Sister Pam makes particularly this day is a profession of Christian life and living as a 'steadfast member of this Order of the Holy Paraclete for life, in the practice of the vows of poverty, celibacy and obedience under the Rule and Constitution of this Order'. Here is a profession of protest – poverty, celibacy, obedience – not entirely qualities of life for which our contemporary society is particularly notable! Yet as well as their important spiritual and moral dimensions and their particular applicability to the monastic way of life, there is surely here a message for the whole Church and for the world.

The challenge of the world's poor is very great. The poor are getting poorer and the rich richer. This is an intolerable situation surely for any Christian. And if the poor are to become richer then it seems to me self-evident that the rich will have to become poorer. It is a considerable challenge to the smug self-satisfaction, self-interest and self-aggrandize-ment of much of our northern hemisphere and Western society. Globalization, if it is to have any reality and any meaning, must surely direct us the more readily and resolutely to the desperate need of the world's poor and spur us and our churches and the world the more to that profligacy and generosity of giving which is in the very heart of God. It is often said that celibacy is a burden – and represents a deeply negative attitude to things physical – not least sex! Of course, our society is fascinated, captivated by, crazy about sex. Celibacy, rather than being negative, is a powerful statement for freedom and for God; that sexuality is not the hedonistic pursuit of sex as an end in itself but rather a celebration of the person God has created each of us to be, where there is infinitely more to sex than sex itself and where in the loving of others both you and they will be drawn ever more deeply, intimately and mysteriously into the depths and heights of the one who first loved us. As that *Rule for a New Brother* puts it so well, to embrace celibacy

> does not mean for you the renouncing of love, contempt for the body ... no, it is the bringing of your potential for love into the new and unlimited fruitfulness of the kingdom ... so you are called to be a witness to love, and its begetter, an encouragement to all who are seeking love's genuine image.

Finally, there is the profession of obedience – again, not particularly popular in an age of rights and individual freedoms. Yet here is reflected in this mutuality of obedience the one towards another – 'the fellowship of mutual trust accepting with generous faith the decisions made by the Community and by those in authority'. And yes, you will, as others have no doubt, grumble, even complain, about decisions – by those in authority! Here again I find considerable common sense and good advice in the *Rule for a New Brother*:

> accept with gratitude the sisters God gives you to go with you on the way ... your task is to serve and uphold one another as members of one body ... so be attentive to each other not in order to dominate or exploit ... and you, accept from your sisters the help you need.

And, of course, spare a thought for the Prioress – she is never likely to please everyone – but then that is not the point; hers is the grave burden and responsibility both of discerning and expressing the mind of the community in changing yet exciting times. Obedience demands, above all, from you all an obedience to God's will and God's way.

It is perhaps a happy coincidence that this day of Pam's profession is also the Church's feast of Hildegard of Bingen, one of the most remarkable creative personalities of the Middle Ages and who has become enormously popular over recent years. The Collect for her feast day prays that we who are (to use her words) 'clothed in the scaffold of creation' might be inspired by the breath of God's spirit – 'open our eyes to glimpse your glory and our lips to sing your praises with all the angels'.

Rejoicing, then, in that love of God which first loved us, we proudly profess the name of Jesus Christ, the one who was dead but who is alive for evermore and in whose risen life we also live and move and have our being, now and in eternity.

Ten

Sermon For All Saints' Day

All Saints, Margaret Street – Sunday, 1 November 1998

'How blessed are those who know their need of God' (Matthew 5.2)

This church of All Saints, as you will know rather better than I, has been variously described – as in one guide to worship in central London – 'From beautiful mystery to tasteless extravagance'; or in Sidney Dark's *Mackay of All Saints* – 'As ugly as it is uncomfortable', or yet again in another comment – 'frozen turmoil'. All this, of course, I hasten to add, of the building rather than the people! But what of the 'saints' of All Saints? What is to be said of all of you? How are you to be described – indeed, is it even possible to embark on so risky and precarious a venture? For myself I judge that silence might be the wiser course! But then I recall that my final sermon as Bishop of this Diocese of London was preached in this church on the occasion of the induction of your new vicar; and I further remember the description of yourselves which you supplied to me and which was to form your new vicar's charge – 'Demanding, intelligent, eccentric, crazy, sad, muddled, confused and, sometimes, part of the holy people of God, but never boring'. I just wonder which of this list your vicar has found to be pre-eminently characteristic and descriptive of the saints of All Saints!

As I survey the long line of the saints who have been

formally named in the Church's calendar I find the diversity and variety of people, women and men, breathtaking in its range; all sorts and types and conditions, and therefore tremendously encouraging – a source of hope for us all; we who feebly struggle whilst they in glory shine. So today on this feast of All Saints, as we contemplate those both named and unnamed who have, as our Salvation Army brothers and sisters so beautifully put it, 'Gone to glory', what do they have to say to us the saints of All Saints, on the verge of a new millennium? If there is one thing writ large in the lives of the saints it is that they came to know their need of God. Here is the very heart of the matter – not only for them, but also for us, for Christians in every age – a recognition of our deep need of God. 'Like as the hart desireth the water-brooks: so longeth my soul after thee, O God.'

In a world of fragmentation and increasing confrontation, where confusions and anxieties abound and where there is much fear about the future, where is it all going? Where surfers and seekers abound, here in the lives of the saints we have sure signposts for the Church in the present and into the future. True enough, they speak to us from the past; not, though, a past which is over and done with. It was the Tractarian revival of an understanding of the Church, not as arm of the state, not simply one organization or institution among others, but rather the Church as a divine society, encompassing, embracing the whole company of the faithful in heaven and on earth, where life today is to be lived and understood in the context of life eternal; a larger, more inclusive, Catholic vision, which in drawing out the past into the present gives us the courage and the confidence to move ahead into the future.

Here in the saints is no roll-call of past heroes. Rather they are our sisters and brothers; they are with us on the way, alongside us as companions and guides, sustaining us with their prayers and guiding us by their example. And it is here in the celebration of these holy and awesome mysteries that in those words of the author of the Epistle to the Hebrews 'We stand before Mount Zion and the city of the living God, heavenly Jerusalem, before myriads of angels, the full concourse and assembly of the first born citizens of heaven and God the judge of all.' What a contrast to that dull, pedestrian, committee-speak and committee-bound utilitarian view of the Church which all too frequently I experience and which is hardly likely ever to inspire or convert anyone to anything.

We desperately need to recover this vision of the Church which is God's and not ours; where we recognize readily the brokenness and sinfulness of our frail humanity, knowing our need of God yet at the same time rejoicing in the abundant mercy and grace of the God who in Christ has come among us and alongside us, who accepts us just as we are, and whose Holy Spirit is already at work in and through each one of us in this sacramental celebration, for transformation and change; changing the dust of all our feebleness, frailty and sinfulness into the gold of His glory.

One of the ways in which so many of the saints are honoured in their search for God is in their scholarship; saints as scholars, disciples in the school of Christ. They have immersed themselves in the Scriptures, in that reflective, digestive reading of the sacred text, that Word of God 'sharper than a two-edged sword ... discerning the thoughts and intentions of the heart'; that Word, 'which is a lantern unto our feet and a light unto our path'.

It was the great names of the Tractarian movement in our own Church who revived for us the writings of the Fathers of the Church, Eastern and Western, typified here in the sanctuary; looking down and keeping an ever-watchful eye on the liturgical celebration. It was our forebears in the movement who opened up the history of the early Church; its life, its witness, its controversies, its worship. Patristic, doctrinal, liturgical and biblical scholarship were all part of the exciting quest and exploration, never in any kind of fundamentalistic way but rather to rediscover the roots of the great tradition – to establish that connectedness and those continuities with and from the past which breathe life and hope into the present for the future.

'The function of the Anglican appeal to antiquity is both faith guarding and identity affirming', writes the former Archbishop of Dublin, Henry McAdoo; and it is in this context that our freedom for exploration and questing and questioning, the academic and intellectual enterprise, must continue to be pursued. It is in that delicate interplay between Scripture, tradition and reason that the Anglican way of doing theology is best typified and identified – a theological method still valid as we seek to engage with difficult and controversial issues which confront and challenge the Church today, as they have in almost every age and from the very beginning, and where listening and dialogue are as important in understanding and learning as they are in resolution and reconciliation.

The real challenge, of course, is to ourselves, each and every one of us, ordained and lay, that we shall so seek to ground and inform ourselves. The learning age – lifelong learning – is surely as applicable to the Christian community as to any other. And there is a vital need for catechesis, for teaching, for learning as a dimension of Christian discipleship to which we all need to attend. What do I believe? And why? And, most important of all, what difference does it make to my life, my decisions, my friendships and relationships, my whole way of life? For if it is about anything, 'Catholic' can never be hijacked in any sectarian, backs-to-the-wall kind of way. Rather it is about seeing things whole – full-face to God and to each other and to the future, with all the excitement, precariousness and risk that that involves.

Saints as signposts for the Church, saints as scholars, and now saints as simpletons; fools for Christ, whose foolishness is the folly of the cross, the scandal of the crucified God. For many of the saints their style and way of life has itself been a challenge to the Church, let alone their utterances or their silence. Phyllis McGinley in her poem about St Simon Stylites catches something of the flavour, as well as the foolishness:

On top of a pillar Simon sat.
He wore no mantle,
He had no hat,
But bare as a bird
Sat night and day,
And hardly a word
Did Simon say.

And why did Simon sit like that,
Without a mantle,

Without a hat,
In a holy rage
For the world to see?
It puzzles me.
It puzzled many
A desert Father,
And I think it puzzled the
Good Lord rather.

Here certainly was protest and there was prophecy too – for the Church and the world. Yes, it was extremist, yet the urgency of the situation demanded it, the Church's accommodation to and with the world which those who went into the Egyptian desert believed demanded extreme measures. Again, it was those priests and lay people, often derided as simpletons and fools by the hierarchy of the day, who in the wake of the Catholic revival deliberately chose to go out into the desert wastelands of the sprawling towns and cities where poverty and oppression were rife, not only to bring people the splendour of the liturgy, but more importantly, in and through the sacramental life of the Church, to nurture in them and for them something of the splendour of their own humanity. Quite rightly the Catholic movement has been strong on the incarnation and incarnation principle – the Mass as the springboard for mission – this celebration of Christ's sacramental presence in the bread of life and the cup of the eternal covenant, sealed in the death and resurrection of Jesus, now actualized and effected in the celebration of Christ's presence in the poor and outcast, the stranger in our midst, each other, our neighbour: 'in as much as you have done to the least of one of these you have done it to me'. It is John Chrysostom who reminds us that 'God has no need of golden vessels but of golden hearts'.

Here is an agenda which takes us quite outside and beyond the Church to the world and its peoples, to the desperate needs and longings of so many; into the heart of those concerns which emerged during the recent Lambeth Conference (and, no, it wasn't all just about sex!). The huge challenge of modern technology with all its possibilities and potential both for life and for death; the widening gap between rich and poor; international debt and economic justice; the violation of women and children; the significance, worth and sanctity of every life; fundamentalism, racism, nationalism; pollution, global warming, ozone depletion and so on. As the report from that particular section comments, 'Many positive, but often complex developments as well as many pressing problems that close this century challenge us to examine our call to full humanity, in Christ Jesus.' And it is that call and its fulfilment in the lives of the saints which we celebrate today: a feast which certainly confronts the mediocre nature of our own discipleship, yet in so doing gives us also the means and the courage to go on. It is the call to holiness, to reject the common sense good and instead opt for the mad best for God – and always and inevitably risk is involved: the risk of breaking out and breaking forth into that eternal and everlasting love which is God's, and which by His mercy and grace can be ours also.

The perspective, then, today must be forwards and onwards. Our forebears in the Catholic movement were zealous for the transformation of the Church and conversion of England. That task remains, and if we are at all to address ourselves to it then we need not only to recover the full meaning of 'Catholic', in the sense of wholeness and inclusiveness, rather than issue-driven and exclusive, quite irrespective of whether we consider ourselves to be of the affirming, traditional, integrity variety or any other for that matter. All of us are Christian, and it is as Christians in these islands today that we are being called to look to the vast and increasing numbers of folk for whom the Christian message is either of little importance or simply irrelevant.

The thrust of this Eucharist is to go out, to go forth, to love and serve the Lord, to go with confidence and joy in the name of the risen and living Lord Jesus Christ and ourselves live his risen life, surrounded as we are by so great a cloud of witnesses, and ourselves to be the instruments of the Lord's love in bringing others to faith, to a knowledge and love of the Saviour; yet all the time keeping alive that vision of the Church which was so dear to those who have gone before us and with whom in these Holy Mysteries we are united in that love which knows no end, that vision of the Church of Jesus Christ as a divine society, as a wonderful and sacred mystery; truly a home for sinners and a school for saints.

Eleven

Day of Advent Reflection for Clergy at York Minster

Monday, 30 November 1998, St Andrew's Day

[The Greeks came and said] 'Sir, we wish to see Jesus'
(John 12.21)

It is said of that great figure of the evangelical revival of the late eighteenth/early nineteenth centuries, Charles Simeon, that he had this very text so inscribed on his pulpit in Cambridge that every preacher could not escape it! It was a reminder, if such a reminder was needed, of the preacher's task on every occasion. And the context of this text is of course that request, recorded for us in St John's Gospel, immediately following the triumphal entry of Jesus into Jerusalem, made by 'some Greeks' who were among those who had come up to worship at the feast. The crucial point of course for the evangelist in introducing this passage is that immediately following Jesus' acclamation by the Jewish crowd with its Messianic greeting 'Hosanna. Blessed is he who comes in the name of the Lord ... the King of Israel', there is at once the recognition of Jesus by the Gentiles. The 'Sir, we would see Jesus' of these 'some Greeks' is but the promise of many more yet to come. Here then in Jesus Christ is not only the King of Israel but the universal Saviour, the one who after He is lifted up will draw all people to Him.

The point of the narrative, of course, is that they do actually get to see Jesus. No doubt they came to Philip because he bore a Greek name and came from a particularly Gentile area and because he also spoke Greek. Philp uncertain himself of how to respond to such a request, consults his fellow disciple (the two seem to have worked as a team at least at one stage). Andrew has no hesitation whatsoever, he leads them to Jesus: 'The hour has truly come for the Son of Man to be glorified.'

What then are the possible implications of this request by these 'some Greeks' for those of us who have been appointed to and entrusted with a ministerial office in the Church of God? Does this narrative, this request, have anything for all of us gathered together this day as we wait upon God in worship and prayer, in penitence and faith, for reconciliation and renewal. I would suggest that perhaps there are three areas where we might find it profitable further to reflect and not least on this feast day of St Andrew – Andrew, disciple, apostle and martyr – the one who, in this narrative at least, opens the door to the Gentiles. The first and most obvious point is, I suggest, the very reason why the evangelist has included these verses at this particular and significant point in his entire Gospel narrative. For it is to do with that question which lurks perhaps in some very inarticulate and inchoate way in the hearts and minds of so many people in our own as in every society.

It is a question about ultimacy – the ultimate meaning – the final destiny of me and my life – of all things. There are very many people who are seeking for something 'they know not what', troubled, anxious about themselves, their lives, their loved ones, their children, their children's children. What is the purpose of it all? Where is it all going to end? And the challenge, of course, is to the Church – how are we to respond? How is it possible even to be in touch with such questions and people? I suppose at heart it is, of course, the very basic question about evangelism and evangelization. Again, what is your response and mine to the request of those beyond and outside our churches and who come to us with their various versions of 'we wish to see Jesus'? Vicar, I want to have him done! It strikes me that there are still so many and varied opportunities through what are termed the occasional offices, when that albeit inarticulate, even begrudging request is made to us and of us – that there is in every such approach at least the seed of a 'We wish to see Jesus.'

So there is first of all here a challenge to us not to turn

Christian faith, Christian conversion, Christian discipleship into a ghetto. It is a reminder of that parochial principle to which our Church remains committed, signalling an availability to and for all. Rather we are to be always alert and aware to the possibility that out there in the many contexts and situations in which we find ourselves – and many of them are 'secular' – in the world, that request 'We wish to see Jesus' will be there also. What is our response?

But then this desire to 'see Jesus' is surely at the very heart of our own vocation: the giving of ourselves, body, mind and spirit, to His service so that as the Ordinal puts it, 'daily we follow the rule and teaching of our Lord and with the heavenly assistance of His Holy Spirit we may grow up into his likeness and sanctify the lives of all with whom we have to do'. However, it is in contrast all too easy in doing the job, in responding to the many calls on your time and your energies – and I am very much aware of the additional pressures and stresses and strains which there are upon us all in one way or another these days – to forget to attend to your own discipleship and apostleship, your own daily following the rule and teaching of our Lord.

One of the purposes of our gathering here today is because I am very mindful that the ministry which we exercise is a shared ministry – 'receive the cure of souls which is both yours and mine'. I am myself also only too well aware of the way in which all the 'doing' – administrative, pastoral, social, ecclesiastical – including the prayer and the worship aspects of our ministry – how all of this can if we are not careful become simply the doing of it; going through the motions; getting on with it and through it, solely for the sake of it. Meanwhile the inner life slowly but surely becomes that barren and dry land described by the psalmist 'where no water is'. I am mindful of the powerful reflections of Archbishop Lang as he considered his twenty years or so at York and which some of you may recall I shared with you when I first came among you as archbishop three years or so ago now:

I look back in these notes to the beginning of my time as Archbishop of York and think of all the hopes and plans with which I began. And now after twenty years the ending.

Certainly there was enough and to spare of doing. Yet, after all the ceaseless process of doing, what was done? Again I cannot tell. God knows. Church life somewhat encouraged and invigorated, I hope; ... how many souls were brought nearer to God by all this doing? The words of the Methody hymn come to my mind – doing is a very deadly thing. What is certain is that much more of true value might have been done if I had cared less for doing and more for being. If the inner life had been kept more true, the outer life would have borne more fruit: "he that abideth in me and I in him", saith the Lord, "the same bringeth forth much fruit: for apart from me you can do nothing".

Here I believe are very timely words also for all of us, not least as we face these weeks and days before Christmas. Use today as an opportunity, then, to reflect on your own inner life and the priority in terms of time and opportunity which you give to the deepening of your own relationship with, and love of, the Lord, when you yourself are able to respond to that longing in your own heart – 'I wish to see Jesus.' Again as the Ordinal puts it, you will need to

pray earnestly for God's Holy Spirit ... pray that each day that he will enlarge and enlighten your understanding of the Scriptures, so that you may grow stronger and more mature in your ministry as you fashion your life and the lives of your people on the Word of God.

It is significant that on each of the occasions in the Gospels in which Andrew appears he is on each occasion bringing someone to Jesus. Another place in the Johannine narrative where Andrew is mentioned is in the feeding of the five thousand in chapter six – which of course leads on to that magisterial meditation on Jesus, the bread of life. You will recall that the huge crowd has assembled to hear his teaching. The day draws on and the people are hungry. The prospects are in no way promising. Andrew, however, it is who recognizes a lad in the crowd with his packed lunch of five rolls and two small fish. He brings him to Jesus. The hungry crowd are fed. Perhaps there is here something of a model and a pattern for our own ministry – in the context of the Church itself – among those to whom we minister in our congregations and churches. No, we may not have the five thousands. I suspect, though, we have our unpromising situations and people, probably rather more of them than we would wish!

Here, surely, in this particular incident is an encouragement to us to discern the gifts, both of the situation in which we find ourselves and of the people among whom we are set. And I am sure you will all recognize there are immense gifts and riches among us in the persons of those of our people who are ready so willingly and readily to assist us in the ministry and mission entrusted to us. It is our task to serve them with joy and build them up in the faith – to encourage them in the places where they live and are, to 'be' as salt and light. The five loaves and two fish in the context of the feeding of the five thousand are also a reminder to us that 'with God nothing is impossible' – even our weakness, our failures, our vulnerabilities He takes, He transforms and uses for His purpose. Thank God that He does make so much out of so little, my meagreness and my begrudging. But then it is all grace – the amazing and totally overwhelming wonder of God's mercy and God's grace which alone can sustain and uphold us in this ministry which is both yours and mine.

As, then, this day we come together for this thanksgiving to God, the Lord is here – 'where two or three are gathered together in my name there I am in the midst of you' – he addresses and challenges us in his Word and he feeds us with the Bread of Life and the Cup of the New Covenant. Do not our hearts burn within us? Pray then for each other, for our Diocese, its bishops, clergy and its people, and for all who do not know the Lord Jesus Christ – and not least for ourselves, that we may know Him more clearly, love Him more dearly and follow Him more nearly, day by day.

Twelve

St Thomas's Church, New York

Sunday, 7 November 1999

'When Jesus saw the crowds, he went up the mountain ... then he began to speak' (Matthew 5.1–2)

The Mount of the Beatitudes is one of the most beautiful places in the Holy Land. The vistas are wide and open as one looks across the lake to the Golan Heights beyond. Here Jesus most certainly walked; here the fishermen are still to be seen, mending their nets, doing their fishing. And here on one of the hillsides surrounding the lake is the place where Jesus addressed the crowds: hillsides to which he would retreat for periods of stillness, silence and reflection. This, then, is the setting, the context in which Matthew places what has come to be known as the Sermon on the Mount. The Beatitudes with which the Sermon begins have gained a universal appeal. They cross the boundaries of denominations and faiths. Our Lord's words in these opening verses of the fifth chapter of St Matthew's Gospel have been described as some of the most radical ever written – a manifesto for a revolution! They have certainly been both the inspiration and the vision of many of those whom we commemorate and celebrate as saints down the ages and throughout the world.

In this Sermon on the Mount there is both challenge and contradiction; conflict and confrontation; inspiration and ignominy; encouragement and offence. After all, a closer examination of some of the propositions are pretty preposterous: 'do not resist evil ... if anyone strikes you on the right cheek turn the left ... give to the one who begs from you ... love your enemies ... if your right hand causes you to sin cut if off and throw it away'.

Now who in their right mind would seek to follow quite such extraordinary advice? Indeed, do we not rather eschew such advice and live our lives entirely contrary to those precepts which are here set out so clearly? Do we not have here an impossible ideal – standards of behaviour, a style of life and living which is so impossible that it hardly seems worth making any effort even to attempt to follow the guidance which the Sermon on the Mount offers to us. One renowned New Testament scholar, Joachim Jeremias, writes

> When we read the Sermon on the Mount we are of necessity moved to despair. Jesus demands that we should free ourselves from anger; even an unfriendly word is to be reckoned as murder. Jesus demands a chastity that extends even to the avoidance of the impure look. Jesus demands absolute truthfulness ... who lives like this? Who can fulfil these demands? Who can live like this?

– so the questions of the commentator.

I rather suspect, too, that as we reflect on the lives of the saints, as we look to those who 'now in glory shine', the same questions may very well cross our minds. At the very beginning by the Galilean Sea there is Andrew and James and Peter and John who on hearing the call of Jesus, 'Come ... follow me', Mark tells us 'immediately' left their nets and followed Him. Is there the same 'immediacy' in our following of Jesus Christ? And what about Anthony of Egypt who, Athanasius tells us, on wandering into a church one day quite by chance heard those words spoken by Jesus to the rich young man – 'Go and sell all that you have and give to the poor' – himself went at once and did precisely that. Is there that same sort of ready and willing sacrifice of yielding and response to God's word in our hearts and lives? And what are we to make of Simon Stylites who spent most of his life perched on the top of a stone pillar?

Is there that spirit of reckless mad abandon about our life and lifestyle and our Christian response? Who indeed lives like this? Who can live like this? The lives of the saints seem to present us with this same impossible ideal, and not least as they are depicted in stained glass, in art and icon, poem and music. The 'distance' between them and us who feebly struggle seems impossibly wide, hardly bridgeable in any way. The whole point, however, about our celebration of the saints is that it is not. Indeed quite the opposite. It is that there is every possibility for each and every one of us of this urgent, sacrificial and reckless living for God and each other. It is no different from that love of God to which we are called – with all our heart and mind and strength – and our neighbour as ourselves. The point is that with God the impossible becomes possible – in our weakness is His strength, in our foolishness is His wisdom. We certainly need such standards and ideals before us, for without these there would be nothing either to encourage or inspire. Here, both in the Sermon on the Mount and in the lives of the saints, signs of contradiction is a reflection of the vision of God; God's awesomeness and splendour, God's beauty and goodness; but also in Christ God's mercy and graciousness, God's humility and never ending love for us and for everything he has made.

What then does all this have to say to us in a world on the brink of the third Christian millennium and where there is much confusion and anxiety – a world altogether more dangerously confrontational as those centripetal and centrifugal forces of globalization and petty nationalisms ferment hatred, bitterness and strife in many countries around the world; a world in which the pace and rate of change in almost every aspect of our lives quickens daily; a world in which many thousands of the human family are condemned to lives of grinding poverty, where water and food and a roof over the head is hardly a glimpse on the horizon and where the rise of individualism and self-centredness and self-gratification, the cult of the individual, has become so much the norm that we are almost inured to the needs of others, either near at home or in more distant lands, and to that love of God reflected in love of neighbour.

The Sermon on the Mount is indeed a stark reminder to us of who and what we are as persons: persons-in-community, created in the image and likeness of God. An extraordinary variety and diversity of personality and people are evidenced right here in this great city of New York – a variety and diversity of people which can either seek and strive to work and live for the common good and the flourishing of all or, in abdicating any responsibility for each other, descend into the darkness and chaos of disorder. Further, the Sermon on the Mount is clear that there are absolute values; absolute values from which we most certainly do and will fall short. Values which are spiritual before they are moral because they spring from the source of all good, who is God. Morality without God is meaningless. As one of my great predecessors in the See of York, Archbishop Temple, writes:

> The standard of morals is the mind of Christ; that is our great principle if we are Christians. It will not help you at once to solve each particular problem; it will give you a touchstone ... your moral authority is not a principle, but a Person. It is the mind of Christ.

It is to that person and mind of Christ which is here before us this day in the Scriptures and this Holy Communion to which we need to return again and again. It is the mystery of His incarnation – God with us, among us, alongside us for ever – which must be at the heart of the millennium celebrations. There will be the material things and the outward and visible things. In England, the Millennium Dome, the London Eye wheel, all of which have recently been specially constructed – numerous other buildings and projects, objects and obelisks up and down the country recording the millennium, as well as the parties and the junketing. Yet without that altogether deeper reflection on who and what we are as persons, the nature of our communities and of society as a whole, the health and well-being of the nation, any celebration of the millennium will be but hollow and short-lived. We need to seize the opportunity which the millennium gives to focus again on those norms and values which as well as celebrating our diversity serve to nurture our being and belonging together as friends rather than enemies, as neighbours rather than strangers – to the renewal and re-establishing of what the Chief Rabbi in England, Jonathan Sacks, in his book *Faith in the*

Future describes as 'the bonds of interconnectedness which make up civil society'.

The Sermon on the Mount, the Beatitudes, the lives of the saints – these signs of contradiction are a clarion call to the Church to attend more seriously and urgently to that altogether deeper engagement with the things of God – a simpler lifestyle, a new asceticism which outwardly and visibly demonstrates that urgency, sacrifice and reckless abandonment of ourselves to the mercy and grace of God, for it is only by His grace alone that we are accepted.

And here it is, with us and among us here and now as we hear His holy Word and receive this bread of life and the cup of the New Covenant. He invites us all, unworthy, quite in spite of who and what we are, to this sacred banquet, to this heaven on earth, to the future glory of dazzling splendour already present among us and around us as, saints on earth and saints in heaven, together we are drawn more deeply and wonderfully and gloriously and gracefully into the very heart of God and His love for us and for the entire world which He has made. And behold, it is very good.

Thirteen

St Thomas's Church, New York

Sunday, 7 November 1999

'Then I saw a new heaven and a new earth' (Revelation 21.1)

It was T. S. Eliot who in one of the Four Quartets wrote 'What we call the beginning is often the end. And to make an end is to make a beginning. The end is where we start from.' The Book of Revelation is certainly about an ending, an ending on a grand scale, an ending of that story which had begun with the beginning: the creation by God of the heavens and the earth and all the host of them. And now in the ending is a new beginning – the vision of John into the future – a new heaven and a new earth. One commentator sums up this passage in lyrical terms: 'All through the long story of God's assault on the old corrupt order there have been intimations of immortality; the promises to the conquerors, the white robed multitude, the triumph song of Moses and the lamb, the wedding feast of the lamb and his bride. The clouds of glory hung low over the camp of the true Israel in their wilderness wanderings. Now at last John stands and surveys the promised land – the future.'

With the dawn of the third Christian millennium almost now upon us it is to the future that I would direct your attention this evening and in particular that beginning, the new start which a new year, a new century, a new millennium offers to us all.

It is no coincidence that 'New Start' is the theme which has been adopted by all the Christian Churches in the United Kingdom as we prepare for and move into the next millennium.

Furthermore, it is a new start in three very real and dynamic respects: a new start for the world's poor; a new start at home; a new start with God. They are themes which I commend to you and on which I should like to reflect for a few moments.

A new start for the world's poor – the campaign for the remission of debt among the poorest countries of the world has been gaining momentum for some time now. It received close and extended attention during the course of the Lambeth Conference in Canterbury last year and in conjunction with economic justice forms a significant part both of the Conference Report and its formal resolutions. I will not burden you with figures. They are available and accessible and they tell their own story. There is some hope that powerful governmental forces, together with the worlds of commerce, business and enterprise, are beginning both to hear and to take seriously and indeed act upon the proposition for the relief of debt. It has to be admitted that there are considerable complexities which need to be understood and appreciated. But at heart this is not a matter simply about our understanding of money – it is rather about our understanding of God and His ways.

The Jubilee 2000 Campaign has certainly caught on in England and other parts of mainland Europe – that pressure needs yet to be sustained. And here there is surely a sign of hope for the future, not only for the poor but also for the Churches in the pursuit of that mission entrusted by God to us all: that in the sinking of our differences in order to pursue this single aim – an aim which focuses our attention on the dignity and the well-being of every human person – the Christian world-wide voice is still of enormous and compelling influence and effectiveness. In this context I have been enormously impressed, even in the short time that I have been here, to discover something of the considerable Christian investment in terms of people, resources, money and enterprise in some of the poorer parts of this city – as is the case in Britain – the Church providing a network of care and compassion, friendship and fellowship as well as the more practical realities of medical assistance and social action. A new start at home directs us quite literally to our own homes and neighbourhoods and communities – to the ordering of our own lives and the priorities which govern them. For in the culture and environment which is increasingly noisy, wordy and busy what space and time do we actually make for each other as 'family', as individuals, where that 'sabbath' principle is no negative Sabbatarian restrictiveness, but rather for our freedom, liberty and flourishing. It is the time and space for relaxation, for re-creation; the necessity of ensuring that our work does not become our whole life, that there are opportunities for enjoyment about which we need not feel guilty, because they are of God. Furthermore, this 'sabbath' principle needs to be extended more widely in the nature and style of our living. We are a voraciously consumerist society; can we continue so to devour and to take from our world and its environment without some restraint or return? In other words, what about the future, the stewardship and sustainability of the planet?

Last year's Lambeth Conference also drew attention to what the bishops describe as a 'sabbath feast of enoughness'. We need to heed the call for restraint and to resist the desire for yet more and more. The sabbath, the Lambeth bishops declared, 'must be reinvigorated, not as a nostalgic symbol of a religious past, but as a feast of redemption and an anticipation of the ecological harmony and sustainable equilibrium of Christ's kingdom'. It was on the sabbath day that God rested – a clear sign of the need for restraint and rest on the part of those of us who are made in His image and likeness – a clear agenda for a new start at home.

And then a new start with God. Here the focus narrows more sharply still, to that personal relationship and friendship which is to be nurtured and deepened between oneself and God. It is a call to prayer and the priority of prayer daily in and through which we are given the energy and the strength and the courage to face the vicissitudes of life. And for those who do pray it does not need me to remind you both of the difficulties as well as the rewards. For so often it seems as if God is more absent from us than he is present to us. Yet as Archbishop Michael Ramsey, successively Archbishop both of York and Canterbury, in his own inimitable way used often to say: the important thing is that you want to want to want to pray. So stay with it and keep at it, for you simply never know the surprises which God has yet awaiting each one of you.

Here, then, at the ending is a beginning, the beginnings of a new heaven and a new earth. It is to this new beginning that we are all invited to contribute. It is a call to look forward and look ahead to the future in faith and with hope. We need to remember our future just as much as our past; and as Augustine reminded the uncertain and cautious Christians of his own day we need to develop the capacity to love the future as much as the past.

It is true the future is hazardous and uncertain, for many futurologists have given us predictions which are as dire as they are unyielding. Their words do not make for encouraging reading.

One of the more extravagant and lurid productions currently in circulation in the United Kingdom tells us: 'We are in the final days warn Bible prophecies! ... how to prepare for Judgement Day ... how to guarantee your place in heaven ... how to find loved ones in after life ... Millennium countdown begins!' Now whilst clearly such material is bizarre in the extreme, nevertheless the Church cannot afford to be anything other than severely realistic, for we do not peddle the kind of religion which either relies on the lifeless fundamentalism of the Scriptures nor on the escape into a docetic world of make-believe. Equally the Christian can never be either overcome or overwhelmed, for our faith is in a God not only of past and present but also and especially of the future – our future – the One who in the words of this Revelation to John is both Alpha and Omega, beginning and end, the one who was dead but is alive for ever more. It is that 'aliveness' of those who are risen with Christ that we seek for the 'aliveness' of the world and its people. Remember St Irenaeus – 'The glory of God is a human person fully alive.'

The millennium directs us to the beginning of this new heaven and new earth in the birth of the Saviour. It is not a project for the future but for the here and now, for this and every day. It is the expectation of the fulfilment in reality of that prayer which Jesus himself taught us – that God's kingdom may come 'here on earth as it is in heaven'.

The summons then to us all is that we cannot and should not wait: to that extent those more lurid predictions are at least right in the urgency to which they alert us. The challenge is to all of us to seek to live in such a way that our homes, our neighbourhoods, our society, our whole world might become a better place – the people and place God intended us in the beginning to be. Pray God that we may so frame and fashion our lives and living to this end, the end which is the beginning, a new start, a fresh start for God and, in Him, for each other day by day.

Fourteen

Walsingham Regional Festival

Saturday, 6 May 2000 – York Minster

'And Mary said, Behold, I am the handmaid of the Lord: be it to me according to your word' (Luke 1.38)

One of the most remarkable things about Walsingham is the homeliness of its holiness. On the one hand, not too dissimilar from the numerous other Norfolk villages, yet on the other, a place distinctive, special, unique – England's Nazareth. It is in fact a reflection, a living icon of our Blessed Lady herself. Here was a young peasant girl just like all those others in and around Nazareth yet one who through the overshadowing of the power of the Most High became the mother of the world's Saviour, now celebrated in the well-known lines of the hymnwriter: 'O higher than the cherubim, more glorious than the seraphim, thou bearer of the eternal word, most gracious, magnify the Lord. Alleluia!'

The celebration of this year of Jubilee – 2000 years, more or less, since the birth of Jesus – is a very appropriate opportunity for this event today – itself special, distinctive and unique in its own way. We have not had to make our way to Walsingham – and why could not God have put down the Holy House in some altogether more accessible and convenient place right by the side of the M1, I hear modern pilgrims often question? Walsingham has come to us, to this ancient and venerable minster church of St Peter – a place which itself has been witness to Christian faith and Christian life for some fourteen hundred years, and where a definitive strike for the Christian faith was made when on Easter Day, 12 April 627, Paulinus, the first bishop of York baptized Edwin, King of Northumbria in a hastily erected wooden hut, the first fragile beginnings of this continuing witness to God's grandeur, God's glory and God's presence in our midst.

The narrative of Luke's Gospel which we have heard again this morning, so familiar and yet so profound, is the account of Mary's 'yes' to God. Not a response either forced or cajoled but rather a response in total freedom made gladly, willingly, lovingly and generously. 'Behold, I am the handmaid of the Lord: be it to me according to your word' – a response integral to the saving work of God among us in Jesus Christ. It was that response which began in Mary herself a journey in faith and of faith, a journey which led her like the Son she bore from the manger in Bethlehem outside the inn to the foot of the cross, outside the city walls – a journey of supreme confidence in God and yet a journey of risk, uncertainty and unknowing. Such is the paradox of Christian believing and discipleship, and such too is the paradox of Walsingham – the homeliness of its holiness.

The readiness and generosity of Mary's 'yes' to God must also become the pattern of the Church's response to God in this as in every age. Mary, the figure of the Church, mother of all Christians, sets before us today the clear call to holiness of life – the Church to live and to be the Gospel.

At the heart of the Catholic revival in the last century there was the recovery of the centrality of this eucharistic celebration with the desire for the worship of God in the beauty of holiness. There were struggles, controversies, sharp and keenly felt for so many of those things which today we simply take either for granted or as of right.

The whole point of course of the centrality of the Eucharist was that it should be just that – at the very heart and centre of all that we are and do. That it should become a whole way of life, drawing ourselves and our lives more fully and completely into that self-offering of Jesus Christ made once for all on Calvary's tree. Moreover, this worshipping of God in the beauty of holiness was itself to flow out and beyond – that mystery and wonder of God's love given so abundantly for us here in this Holy Sacrament, lived out in our own lives in the myriad circumstances and situations in which we find ourselves day by day. It is nothing less than the embrace of God's love for us and for the whole human family, that embrace of acceptance and welcome which is so characteristic of Walsingham itself. I mean the whole family, young and old, different backgrounds, traditions, cultures and experiences: for Walsingham is as much about the future as it is about the past and the present. Further, I am enormously impressed by the increasingly large numbers of young people who attend the youth pilgrimage; of the schools who visit the Shrine and make use of its educational facilities; of those young persons who come inquiring, searching and seeking and with no particular faith at all, and yet who in Walsingham discover something of the knowledge and love of God for them which gives purpose and meaning to their lives. Truly a converting experience – the grace of the incarnate Word at work in Walsingham. For the wonderful thing about Walsingham is that like our eternal home it welcomes us with open arms; its hospitality extended to all and for all, inclusive rather than exclusive, for the reconciliation, healing and renewal of all. Walsingham's 'yes' to you and me is a powerful echo of Mary's 'yes' to God. The challenge of today then is that in the patterning and modelling of our lives individually and corporately as Christians – as a Church and as congregations and parishes – there must be at the heart of it all a closer attentiveness to the God who in Christ has called us into His service, in the discipline of daily prayer and the reading of the Scriptures, in our use of the sacrament of reconciliation, in the way we order and conduct our worship, in the prayerful preparation for this Holy Sacrament and so on. Above all there needs to be an ongoing engagement with the basic truths of the Christian faith – a real delight and enthusiasm in learning ever more in a climate which is paradoxically both sceptical and dismissive and yet where there seems to be an increasing interest in and yearning for things spiritual.

As many of you will know I have only just returned late last evening from a visit to the Holy Father in Rome. The visit I found both immensely moving and enormously heartening. It was, I believe, all the more so because I went at his invitation and with his encouragement with the President of the Methodist Conference and similarly the Roman Catholic Bishop of Middlesbrough, Bishop John Crowley. Such an 'ecumenical' visit is a sure sign of that altogether fuller but not yet perfect unity to which we are all called and for which we pray. The three of us, with other church leaders, had been together for prayer and reflection at Ampleforth Abbey in January and more recently just before Holy Week, again in prayer and reflection together.

Walsingham, too, is that place where in the one domain Christians of all denominations come together to honour Mary the bearer of the eternal Word of God. Though our differences are sometimes painfully manifest, there is nevertheless an overwhelming unity in our desire together to worship and witness to the one God and Father of our Lord Jesus Christ and to the truth of the incarnation. We bear patiently and prayerfully with those differences as we seek to respond to Mary's gift to us of her beloved Son and the new life that daily he offers to us and for us. And here surely is a model and a way for us within our own Church when there are differences and disagreements within the family – in our parishes, in the Church at large and where there is a continuing need for respect and courtesy for the exercise of those gifts of the spirit of patience and kindness, of long-suffering and gentleness, that patient endurance so typified in the Blessed Mother whom this day we honour. Such is the homeliness of Walsingham's holiness for us and for our churches, and would that it were more displayed in and among them.

Today, then, in the joy of Christ who is risen we give thanks for all that Walsingham has been and continues to be for us and for so many others the world over – for those who in the face of much scorn and opposition re-established the Shrine and over the years have supported its prayer and its life, its welcome and its witness with such great generosity and faithfulness. We cannot and we shall not continue this saving work in and of our own strength. So it is that today, as we offer these holy and sacred mysteries, we make our prayer together with the whole company of heaven: the glorious company of the apostles, the goodly fellowship of the prophets, the noble army of martyrs and, most specially, with Mary the mother of

God, our Lady of Walsingham, that like her and all those who now in glory shine we may today and every day ourselves respond with our 'yes' to God – in wonder, love and praise.

Fifteen

General Synod

York Minster – Sunday, 9 July 2000

'Whether they hear or refuse to hear (for they are a rebellious house), they will know that there has been a prophet among them' (Ezekiel 2.5)

The person I last saw and heard in this pulpit was Mrs Noah. It was the opening night of the Mystery Plays – and what a contentious and rebellious Mrs Noah she was! In the end she had to be almost literally manhandled by Shem, Ham and Japheth into the ark, thereby ensuring her and their salvation. She resisted like mad, but in the end she made it – and perhaps there is something here for you and me too – resistant as we are to God's will for us as individuals, as a Church and yet saved by His mercy and His grace – so long-suffering, so forgiving, so amazing, so profligate.

And it was of course to a 'rebellious house' – the Church of England – that that report of the Partners in Mission Consultation nearly twenty years ago now was directed. One of my predecessors as Archbishop of York, Stuart Blanch, the Chairman of the Consultation, commented at the time:

> This report will have done its work if it causes subtle, sometimes imperceptible, changes of attitude in official bodies and voluntary societies as they seek to gather their resources around one unifying objective – the mission of the Church to the Nation.

Like many other reports from that day to this, it certainly seemed to cause a bit of a stir at the time, but for the rest –

well it just seems to have disappeared into oblivion. Unpalatable though some of its contents may have been, it was in fact a prophetic document in several respects, not least in the priorities to which it directed our attention at that time. But then as one participant in the consultation commented, 'We are all in favour of change so long as it doesn't make any difference!'

And in this particular context it is of course the prophet Ezekiel, one among that huge number of captives brought from Jerusalem to Babylon and now in exile in an alien and foreign land, in a place of total weakness and vulnerability. This is the context of Ezekiel's prophetic protest. True enough a protest against what he described as a 'rebellious house' which had become impudent and stubborn. But more importantly a prophetic protest *for* the works and ways of God: for God's holiness, for God's righteousness and justice, for God's amazing and abundant grace – the long-suffering generosity and profligacy of God's love even in those moments of utter rebelliousness. And it is to this more positive prophetic protest to which I should like to direct our thoughts this morning – a protest which like Israel of old the contemporary Church needs to hear and respond to. And in concert with the themes on which I have just touched there are, I believe, a number of clear priorities for us today: a priority for prayer, a priority for the poor, a priority for the planet.

It is not altogether insignificant that the beginning of the last millennium saw the Church in some state of disarray to which the response was a clear spiritual renewal – the renewal as it happened of an altogether more austere monasticism such as had been characteristic in its earliest days and forms in the Egyptian desert. Many of the great houses here in Yorkshire were a result of that renewal – Fountains, Rievaulx, Byland and so on. They focused a deep attention on the things of God in the context of a praying and learning community. And it is that praying and learning community which is the vocation of the Church in every age. How well George Herbert puts it:

Prayer the Church's banquet, Angels age, God's breath in man returning to his birth, The soul in paraphrase, heart in pilgrimage. The Christian plummet sounding heaven and earth ... Heaven in ordinary ... Church bells beyond the stars heard, the soul's blood, The land of spices, something understood.

How desperately we need to recover that sense of heaven in ordinary!

Whether it is a survey on Church attendance or on the soul of Britain, one of the clear messages to the Churches is that, to quote a recent article in *The Tablet*, 'The nation is seeking spiritual guidance and the Church is not seen to be providing it.' Maybe we need ourselves to be more attentive to spirituality than to our religiosity and our churchiness – and the claustrophobic nature of our own agendas. How do we respond to the fact that, for example, well before these Mystery Plays opened they were fully booked? One thousand people every night for twenty-five nights drawn into the mysteries of God's work among us in creation, in the birth, death and resurrection of Jesus Christ and in the work of the Holy Spirit and not least the Last Judgement.

Simply to be here is a transforming experience. Perhaps the Synod would have been better occupied, even edified, by abandoning some part of its agenda this weekend to 'be' here! And in a similar vein what of the thousands who came to look with awe and wonder at the image of Christ – that exhibition at the National Gallery earlier this year, 'Seeing Salvation'. Not a word spoken, not a sermon preached, not even a General Synod debate! There are clear messages here for us surely, not only about how we pray but about the manner and style of our worship and about what the mode of that spiritual guidance which so many are seeking might be.

The prophetic protest for the poor is as alive today and in this twenty-first century as it has ever been, and particularly later this month with the forthcoming meeting of the G7 countries in Japan. Jubilee 2000 has been an enormously successful campaign – a sign of what it is possible to achieve on a world-wide scale when the churches and indeed other faith communities really are prepared positively to protest in a concentrated and co-ordinated way. That protest needs yet to be sustained. I know there are the complexities and the intricacies but if we are truly called to a full humanity in Christ then in an increasingly global context we cannot evade the desperate plight of so many of our brothers and sisters who are one with us in that family created in the image and likeness of God.

The real question before us is, of course, after the example of the One who though He was rich yet for our sakes became poor. Are we prepared to be the poorer so that the poorest may be the richer? And that is an equally appropriate question for us all in the parishes, the places where we are, in terms of our contributions, our attitudes and our giving. Are we prepared to bear one another's burdens within deanery and diocese and so fulfil the law of Christ? The real challenge of the prophetic protest for the poor is, as the Churches Together identified for this millennial year, nothing less than a new start. Intimately and inextricably bound up with the priority for prayer and for the poor is the priority of the prophetic protest for the planet. This holistic view of things is very much a part not only of a thoroughgoing Christian doctrine of creation but of Celtic Christianity, and was brought home to me personally again very clearly in leading the Church Army pilgrimage to Lindisfarne. One of the greatest contributions of Celtic Christianity was the way in which those patterns and designs figure so prominently in the art, sculpture and architecture of those days. Those wonderfully intricate patterns which weave their way in and out and around and through, often using birds and fish and trees and flowers, are a powerful statement about God's lordship over the whole of creation and a clear challenge to our stewardship of it. It showed, too, that there could be no distinction between the spiritual and material – that we are all of a piece. They didn't need any green agenda or green lobby or even Green Party. They were themselves only too well aware of the sheer wonder and glory and diversity of God's creation and the need to tend it and care for it and nurture it. Those funny stories, for example, about the otters which warmed the feet of St Cuthbert and then dried them with their fur when he had been out dipping in the North Sea, and one of Columba's followers whose only companions in his solitude were a cock, a mouse and a fly – the cock crowing at midnight to wake him for Matins, the mouse nibbling at his ear to wake him for the day and the fly walking along the lines of his Bible! These speak to us powerfully of the fundamental unity of all things in God's creation. How we need to attend to this priority for the planet, and particularly at a time when there is a serious concern for the sustainability of so much of our natural heritage and the very future of the earth itself! How right Lambeth 98 was when it called for a reinvigoration of the concept of 'sabbath', not as a nostalgic symbol of a religious past, but as a feast of redemption and an anticipation of the ecological harmony and sustainable equilibrium of Christ's kingdom!

It is, of course, in this very eucharistic celebration that we honour the sacramentality of all things, for this is the feast of the kingdom, *the* moment of God's profligate love and amazing grace not only for each of us but for the entire created order. Here is no celebration either for the pious few, for the holy club, for the straightest sect. There is no place here for exclusivity. Rather, in that great feast of God's kingdom of which this Eucharist is both sign and promise I suspect we may all be rather surprised by whom we shall find already there. As Harry Williams so amusingly narrates: 'Athanasius and Arius laughing together at the absurdity of their theological definitions; or Augustine and Pelagius slapping each other on the back instead of in the face'. It is in fact a celebration of the triumph of God's mercy and grace over the rebellious house that is both ourselves and our Church – the God who is in all and through all and over all – the God who even now all unworthily invites each of us to this feast of life – a foretaste of those good things which he has yet in store for us eternally and everlastingly.

To the same God and Father of our Lord Jesus Christ be all praise and thanksgiving now and to the end of the ages. Amen.

Sixteen

Service of Celebration for the Northern Province of the Church of England

York Minster – Thursday, 27 July 2000

'If anyone is in Christ, he is a new creation; the old has passed away, behold, the new has come' (2 Corinthians 5.17)

It was John Wesley who in riding into these northern parts noted in his Journal: 'A wilder people I never saw in England. The men, women and children filled the streets as we rode along – and seemed just ready to devour us!' Well, they did not. And I hope that if Wesley were to make the same journey today then he would write a somewhat more positive note in his Journal, especially on this day when we celebrate the life of the Northern Province of the Church of England, together with so many of our ecumenical guests present – pilgrims together on the same journey of faith. The bellicose nature of the north, implied in John Wesley's Journal was, of course, a reality for long enough between the two Provinces, Northern and Southern, especially in what might be described as the conflict of the crosses. Which of the archbishops was able – had the right – to carry his primatial cross in the Province of the other? Feelings ran very high at times, even to the point of the crosses themselves being deployed as instruments of aggrandisement and aggression – chiefly it has to be admitted on the part of the north! The whole matter was finally sorted by an Instrument dated 20 April 1353 bearing the seals of both archbishops but with the concluding concession, that whilst the two arch-bishops should always seek to walk/process side by side, yet if they should find themselves confined in a narrow passage then the cross of York should defer to that of Canterbury. If ever you wanted to know, that's something, at least, of the difference between what it means to be Primate of England and Primate of All England!

Our celebration today gives us the opportunity in this majestic Minster with its newly restored western front – the result of many years of prudent planning and ardent fund-raising by the York Minster Fund chaired by the Minster's High Steward, the Earl of Halifax, and to which so many have so generously contributed – to give thanks for the Christian heritage into which we are entered, in which we live, and which bears us forward and onward into the future. There are three names in particular from the earliest of days I should like to set before you this morning. For although they come to us from the distant past, their voices and their lives are particularly relevant for the whole Church as we embark on this twenty-first century.

The first is Paulinus. It was of course Pope Gregory who had earlier sent Augustine to establish the Christian mission in the south who now directed Paulinus and his four companions northwards, bearing with them a missive from him to Augustine in which his intentions were signalled that York should be a metropolitan see with twelve suffragans. Paulinus' stature according to Bede was striking: black hair, vivid eyes and of meagre cheek! Here was a missionary prepared to take risks: to leave the comfort and the safety of his own home, his own place, his own country and in obedience to the Lord's command to go and preach the Gospel, to make disciples of all nations. He found himself in an alien culture and among a hostile and pagan people. Even after the memorable conversion of Edwin and so many of his kinsfolk, Paulinus did not remain simply with the converted. Like the apostle Paul before him, and indeed as with many of the northern saints, they spent their time going from place to place, from village to village, as it was said of Cuthbert: 'preaching the way of truth to those who had gone astray, and calling them heavenwards by his example'.

The same call to mission remains an urgent task for the Church today. An evangelization of engagement and service rather than of arrogance and assertiveness; a readiness to take risks and move out of the confines of our churchiness and religiosity into the territory of those of today who seem to have heard the name of Jesus Christ only as a curse rather than a blessing. And it will only be by that personal engagement on the part of each and every one of us, that clarity of purpose, perseverance in faith and style of life, so typified by Paulinus – his readiness to be with and among both the highest and the lowest, the richest and the poorest – which can again be fruitful for the Christian mission today.

Another figure is that tongue-tied herdsman Caedmon, a member of Hilda's monastery at Whitby, deeply envious of the others who sang so melodiously and well when he could not. Yet in the end he excelled them all with his Song of Creation:

Now must we praise Heaven's Ward, the Lord's might and His intentions – work of the Glory-Father – He each wonder ordered – Eternal Lord – First Creator – He first made – for children of old – heaven as a roof – Holy One created – this Middle-Earth – Mankind's Guardian – Eternal Lord – after created – for men a country Praise the Almighty.

We could not have a more direct or potent challenge to a Christian care for creation, that stewardship entrusted right at the very beginning to the human race as the high priests of all creation. A world not to be disfigured, raped and ravaged by the greed and selfishness of human kind, but rather to be tended and nurtured and cared for so that its resources may be conserved and sustained for generations yet to come. Caedmon's song is reflected well in Gerard Manley Hopkins' 'Pied Beauty': 'The world is charged with the grandeur of God.' The Churches must be determined to become more actively involved in issues of conservation. Already, I am glad to say, following the very successful launch of the Year of the Millennium initiative with David Bellamy here in York, many parishes remain in touch with the Conservation Foundation precisely to such an end.

No longer – if ever it was true – is northern England, either side of the Pennines, an area of unremitting dark satanic mills. The scars are certainly there and the wounds remain in many communities, but equally we are blessed with some of the most dramatic and beautiful countryside in the whole of the British Isles. The rural areas and the farming communities need and deserve our strongest support at this time. For their communities, like the miners and the shipbuilders, the weavers of wool and the spinners of cotton before them, are now in crisis. Care for our communities just as much as care for creation must be a priority for us all, the one is inseparable from the other.

Already I have touched on that most formidable of all women in those early days, Hilda of Whitby. She even managed to knock some sense into the contentious disputes of the bishops at the Synod of Whitby in 644, a synod which was to alter the course of church history in these islands for good. Her presence among the array of northern saints bears testimony to the contribution which women have made not only to the life of the Church but to the life of our communities more widely, to the towns and villages of northern England – women not only in the home but in the workplace, women of enterprise and skill, women of perseverance, courage and heroism. Furthermore, given a mixed community both of men and women, here, for Hilda at least, was a reflection of God's glorious creativity – that profligate diversity yet harmonious complementarity of women and men, the society of the saints in heaven already mirrored here on earth. Bede sings the praises of her virtues: virtues so much needed in our society today – justice, devotion, chastity, peace, love. Yet beyond all this is the long physical illness which afflicted her for some six years before her death and which she bore with such remarkable fortitude. Her death was witnessed in a vision by one of her sisters: Hilda's soul ascending to heaven in the company of the angels.

And it is this vision of the eternal, of that life beyond this life, the hope of heaven which must continue to inform our vision and our lives. Furthermore, in a society where death seems to be such a taboo here we are presented with this stark reality of our own weakness, fragility and mortality yet at the same time with God's strength made perfect in our weakness and the sheer wonder and beauty of God's glory into which already daily we are being drawn ever more deeply, 'changed from glory into glory till in heaven we take our place'.

You may not have noticed it, but it is the saints of the north who are depicted beneath the primatial cross of York. Like the cross borne ahead and before, so they along with the crucified and risen Lord have gone ahead and before and continue so to do. Today, in the first months of this new millennium, they beckon you and me forwards. They encourage us onwards towards the bright hope of God's future for us and for the entire human family.

Seventeen

Service for Yorkshire Day

Tuesday, 1 August 2000 – York Minster

'This is the day which the Lord has made; let us rejoice and be glad in it' (Psalm 118. 24)

One of the most fascinating and interesting aspects of my ministry as archbishop, as indeed I suspect those of you who serve in public office will readily recognize, is the sheer diversity of the people I meet and the places to which I am invited. Within the space of about one week, for example, I can find myself at the Great Yorkshire Show, at the York Races, addressing a group of business executives on the subject of business ethics – Does Virtue Pay? – and, on the whole, I wasn't sure that they thought it did! Presenting awards to apprentices on an engineering and technical course, and visiting the classes of a primary school in a deprived urban area – taking my 'bishop's clothes', as they call them, and then waiting for the questions – almost fatal, of course, with youngsters: 'Please, sir, do you use hair gel?'

I look back over the lives and work of former archbishops and whilst, of course, much has changed – and change itself, rapid and perplexing and daunting is very much a part of life's fabric today, on the other hand, I conclude sometimes after some visits very little has changed! I am reminded of the note which Archbishop Lang in the early 1900s made in his diary about a visit he had made to one of the rural parishes here in Yorkshire:

On one occasion, visiting a parish in the East Riding wolds I found two churchwardens, one aged about 75 and the other about 85 and almost wholly deaf. They evidently regarded me and my business with some suspicion. I began to get on well with the younger man, which only increased the suspicions of his older and deaf colleague. Suddenly the latter asserted himself and said: "If tha's come here for money, I tell thee there's nowt to be had." Then having faithfully given his testimony, he relapsed into silence.

I myself remember earlier this year, again visiting one of our delightful rural churches, and being the son of a builder father I tend to notice these things, spied what I thought looked like a bush sprouting out of the church tower at a fairly high level, and indicated to the person accompanying me that really something ought to be done about it. His immediate response was 'Ee'Archbishop you should come here in the summer. It flowers a real treat!'

One of the books which I have still from my earliest days is *The Country Life Picture Book of Yorkshire* — all black and white photographs – but a book which shows off the sheer scale, variety and beauty of the Yorkshire landscape. Its preface begins: 'There are more acres in Yorkshire, so the saying goes, than letters in the Bible and it is only right that Britain's largest county should have a *Country Life Picture Book* devoted entirely to it.' Similar sentiments are to be found in James Herriot's *My Yorkshire* where he writes,

I think the exact moment when it dawned on me that Yorkshire was a magical place was when I pulled my car off the unfenced road which leads from Leyburn over Bellerby Moor to Grinton ... I gazed at the scene with unbelief ... there was everything here ... I got out of the car ... I was captivated ... completely spellbound and I still am to this day.

An experience which surely will well resonate with all of us here. Often early on a Sunday morning as I drive out from York, in whatever direction, I simply cannot believe how fortunate and blessed I am to be travelling through such remarkable landscapes.

But then, in contrast there is another book on my shelves

given me as I was leaving the Diocese of Wakefield – *Made in Huddersfield* – Jack Ramsey's vivid autobiographical account of a decade of change which has overtaken the industrial landscape of those parts of the West Riding of Yorkshire. Indeed, I was myself reminded of what that huge swathe of industrial Yorkshire must have been like when ten days ago now I took the Trans Pennine Express – transpennine it may be, express by no stretch of the imagination could it ever be! Through Leeds and Batley, on then to Dewsbury and Huddersfield, up the Colne valley through Slaithwaite and into the tunnel at Marsden – at one point there was the Titanic Mill now abandoned on the valley floor as a potent symbol of that thriving but costly (in terms of people and their lives) industrial life of the West Riding. Indeed, I remember often going with my father to Paton and Baldwin's woollen mills in Thornes, Wakefield, and the noise and clatter of the machines – the oily wooden beam floors and the smell of the wool – all now gone and gone for ever – as indeed with much of the steel industry in and around Sheffield and, of course, not least the coal mining industry. The scars and the wounds are still there, they are still visible, both in landscape and people.

Today, Yorkshire Day, here in this majestic Minster at the very heart of Yorkshire – a Minster which itself hosts so much and so many of Yorkshire's life in the course of any one year – gives us the opportunity to rejoice in and celebrate our heritage in this present day and pray to God for his grace and his blessing upon our future together. And at the heart of our celebration must be the people throughout our county and region, not least those living in the rural areas and the farming communities under so much pressure and stress at this present time. Yet true to that sturdy grittiness which has sustained every community, be it urban or rural in times of crisis, endeavouring to keep up and keep going is very much a dimension of these communities today. One of the most striking things about the Great Yorkshire Show was not only the diversity and excellence of products made here in Yorkshire, but the sheer resilience and cheerfulness in adversity of some of those farmers and their families who have been hit so hard. That community spirit which certainly typifies this county continues to serve us well. Yet in an age of increasing individualization, of self-interest, self-promotion, self-protection – basically sheer selfishness – all of us need to work hard to ensure that we remain ready to bear one another's burdens, to rejoice with those who rejoice and weep with those who weep, contributing to the needs of others, practising that hospitality and generosity which again is so much of the Yorkshire spirit. We need these human and civic virtues if we are at all to remain a humane society. Good neighbourliness was certainly very much a part of the neighbourhood in which I myself grew up. Nosiness about other people's business could sometimes become over-intense and indeed over-intrusive. Nevertheless, it ensured that more formal neighbourhood schemes were never really necessary. You not only minded your neighbour, you minded about your neighbour. 'Yorkshire Forward', the strategy document from the Regional Chamber, quite rightly identifies one of the greatest assets of Yorkshire – our people – talented, trustworthy, hard working, and the question before us is how is it possible, given all the advantages, not being blind to the difficulties, the challenges, inadequacies and the weaknesses, further to release and enhance the potential of all who live in this region, not least our young people. They are enormously yet variously talented with energy, enthusiasm and determina- tion. Much more needs to be done for them, particularly for those still in areas of rural and urban deprivation, in developing their educational and vocational skills, and that is an enterprise not just for the schools but for us all. Learning is lifelong – it's an exciting adventure. In a fast-moving and changing world we need to develop those skills and aptitudes whereby how we learn and what we learn can be geared more to a culture which is altogether more readily flexible than it is immovably fixed.

It is surely the constellation of so rich an environment and landscape as well as our people which has made Yorkshire famous the world over for so many things: art and architecture, literature, poetry and music, in the huge cultural, ethnic and religious mix which now forms part of who and what we are. If we are truly to build on such enormous potential then it will require us to encourage enterprise and promote partnerships of the widest possible kind where the public and private sectors will not be working against each other but, rather, with each other in securing the best interests of all. Furthermore, we should not underestimate the huge and considerable contribution which so many individuals, groups and organizations make on a purely voluntary basis, including the Churches and the faith communities, towards that altogether greater flourishing of people, of mind, body and spirit, without which our communities, our region as a whole would be vastly impoverished. So on this first Yorkshire Day of the new millennium we have much to celebrate, giving thanks to God for our past as confidently we commit and commend ourselves and our endeavours to him for the future.

Perhaps the quality above all else onto which we need to hold is that Yorkshire sense of humour, that laughter and fun not so much at others or at the expense of others but with others and at ourselves. Here, it seems to me, is the greatest strength: the ability to laugh at oneself, that laughter which penetrates the pride of a conceited self regard and which itself is a sign of the absurd. A recently widowed husband ordered his wife's gravestone requesting for the inscription, 'Lord she is thine.' He returned to inspect the stone. It read 'Lord she is thin.' 'Tha's missed off the 'e'', he complained. 'Don't worry' responded the stonemason, 'we'll soon put that right, come back next week.' He did and the line then read 'E'lord she is thin.' The lifeline of laughter remains, thank goodness, a source of strength in our weakness and of solace in our sadness. It serves, too, as a very necessary and humanizing virtue to complement that equally necessary northern sturdiness, determination and awkwardness, itself a sign of God's good grace and mercy down the years and with us still.

So as we look to the future with all that has been entrusted to us and the enormous possibilities and potentialities before us, we pray that we may truly live in harmony one with another, seeking ever and always for the flourishing of every human person in our midst and the building up the more of our communities, both rural and urban, so that 'Yorkshire Forward' is no longer simply a slogan but a vision in reality already in our midst and for the good of all.

Eighteen

Service of Thanksgiving for the Restoration of the St William Window

York Minster – Saturday, 9 September 2000

'You are God's own people ... in order that you may proclaim the mighty acts of him who called you out of darkness into his marvellous light' (1 Peter 2.9)

The new millennium has already been celebrated in a wide variety of ways both secular and sacred. The churches, properly and appropriately, have played a very significant part, nationally and locally, in marking the dawn of the third Christian millennium, and this majestic and magnificent Minster is no exception.

In the exercise of my work and office as archbishop it has been both my privilege and pleasure to attend and participate in thanksgivings for initiatives – some major, some quite minor, but no matter, for they are all of considerable significance – taken by churches, urban and rural, spurred on by the new millennium. New bells and ringing chambers, extensions to churches to accommodate new and growing numbers of worshippers, imaginative re-orderings and restorations, a new piece of artwork or sculpture, new social facilities, new music commissioned and new or restored windows dedicated. All in the name and in honour of the one born in a manger because there was no room for him in the inn, all of them proclaiming the mighty acts of the God who in

Christ has called us out of darkness into His own marvellous light.

We celebrate and give thanks for the restoration of the St William Window here in this Minster. And given the fact that as William Fitzherbert sought to clear his name of, among other things, simony and immorality he was denounced publicly in Rome as 'the Idol that the Whore of Winchester (the then bishop in league with the king) had set up in St Peter's Minster', and that he was banished from his archbishopric for some seven years and finally poisoned, allegedly by the Archdeacon of York (Archbishops of York have always been very wary of their archdeacons ever since – even the Dean of York may have been involved given his opposition to William's restoration), it's surprising that there should be any window in his memory at all. Perhaps all the upheaval, the politicking and the turmoil might have been best left consigned to the silence of the past. And indeed, had it not been for the collapse of the Ouse Bridge on William's restoration to the archbishopric in 1154 this may well have been so. However, such was the tumult of the huge crowds of the clergy and laity to welcome him that, though the bridge did indeed collapse under the weight of numbers, by the prayers of William it is said not one was harmed, not a life was lost. A miracle had been performed before their very eyes. The people had witnessed powerfully and presently one of those mighty acts of the God who called them out of darkness into His own marvellous light. Such was the influence of that event that William received almost instant canonization, though not finally and formally until 1227 and, with many miracles attested, finally his mortal remains were enshrined in this Minster church with great pomp in the presence of King Edward I on 9 January 1283.

The St William Window is, of course, but one of a number of unique, distinctive and historic windows here in this great Minster, each of them with their own story to tell, each installed with and for a specific purpose, many of them attesting the finest skills of the York School of Glaziers and Glass Painters. The stained glass here is as ancient, varied and significant as any in the land, indeed throughout Europe. The fact that those of you here this morning have so generously contributed to this restoration is a sign of your commitment that the heritage of the past should continue as a living and lively sign in this present and for the future. Many of the windows tell, of course, of *the* Great Story – that which is so wonderfully and completely narrated in the great east window, amazingly completed in three years and dominated at its apex with God enthroned in glory and the text *Ego sum Alpha et Omega*. And it tells of everything from the beginning to the end, from creation to apocalypse. And, of course, that is why there are so many such windows in so many of our churches – they were quite literally an illustrated Bible. They served for instruction and teaching, for education and learning.

Many of the great west windows of our churches contain scenes of the Last Judgement, and grotesquely literalist they are in their representations of hell. It was a severe warning to those departing from divine worship that they had better order their lives accordingly or else that same fate would await them, perhaps rather sooner than they imagined! Similarly, the windows such as the St Cuthbert and the St William Windows were for the purposes of exhortation and encouragement, still very relevant for us in the twenty-first century as in the twelfth. For although, of course, much around us changes and continues to change at a rate of alarming rapidity, it would appear that human nature itself changes very little. The experiences of life – its surprises and its successes, its struggles and its frustrations, its disappointments and its joys, all that which is the experience of you and your life – is not much different from the human experience of those of generations past; hence the key relevance of that which we are about this morning. The St William Window addresses us now as it did then and as it will continue to do into the future, thanks to your generosity and beneficence. It continues to exhort and encourage, to strengthen and support us on our journey of faith, on our way through life, setting before us as it does the sure triumph of good over evil; of light over darkness, the supreme power of the God who has created us and in Christ redeemed us – the God who even now calls you and me out of darkness into His own marvellous light. You will be aware, of course, that the St William Window was originally a gift of the De Ros family from Helmsley Castle, itself an act of charity. Today your charity and that of your colleagues has ensured this window for the future.

Now I use the word 'charity' advisedly, for that is precisely what it is. It is a word not to be belittled or demeaned or despised, for at its very heart it speaks of love. Moreover, it reminds us of that love which God has for his world and for all he has created – yourself and myself included. Its a virtue which appeals to our higher human nature, a word which speaks at the same time both of sacrifice and of generosity. It is, in short, that charity which in those noble and memorable words of St Paul is 'not envious or boastful or arrogant ... it does not rejoice in wrong-doing but rejoices in the truth ... that charity which bears all things, believes all things, hopes all things, endures all things' – such charity which can never fail.

Here, then, is a virtue which is for all – Christian and non-Christian, believer and non-believer, agnostic and atheist. It is a challenge to our lives and way of living day by day. It is an appeal to our better and higher human nature, to that care and compassion which we extend to our neighbour whoever that neighbour may be, an invitation to let your light so shine before men that they may see your good works and glorify your Father which is in heaven. I rather think that if this were the guiding principle of people everywhere then the world would undoubtedly be a very different place, and much for the better too.

Perhaps, then, we could do no better than at the beginning of this new millennium and on this occasion in particular to reflect more deeply and carefully on those very basic spiritual and moral principles on which we live our lives and which determine our decisions, our reactions; our present and our future. Reflection is one thing, action is another, for both our readings this morning – the one of Solomon in the magnificence of the Temple, the other of Peter to a group of young Christians – are the same, namely, the recognition of God's lordship over all and the consequences of that recognition particularly at a time and in an age when idols of one sort or another abound.

The consequence of that first and great commandment, our commitment to the love of God with heart and soul and with mind and with strength, is an equal commitment to each other, love thy neighbour as thyself. The two are inseparable, and again, together at the beginning of this new millennium, they invite us to a way and style of life which God wills for all.

As then we give thanks to God and re-dedicate this window to His praise and glory so may we re-dedicate ourselves, our souls and bodies, our whole lives, that we like blessed William and all the saints may live our lives ever in His service and always to His praise and glory. To the same God be all praise and thanksgiving now and to the end of the ages. Amen.

Nineteen

St Stephen's House Reunion

St John's Church – Monday, 11 September 2000

Stephen, 'full of the Holy Spirit, gazed into heaven and saw the glory of God, and Jesus standing at the right hand of God' (Acts 7.55)

For those of us who did our training when the House was at Norham Gardens, the martyrdom of Stephen was a daily recurrence. There, morning by morning, day by day, before your very eyes in that tunnel-like chapel, you beheld the stoning of Stephen – all the more obvious after the Hope reformation than before it, when for the most part it had been obscured by what are commonly called 'the big six', now reposing on the high altar of this church. It had certainly not been my object, I hasten to add, the more to expose that mural to the vulgar gaze. Indeed, when we moved here from Norham Gardens I would happily and readily have lost it altogether in the removal – mysteriously of course! But one or two Governors insisted on its coming here. It is, I think, now in one of the furthest reaches of the House, in the small chapel at the top of Benson, and perhaps that is really the best place for it! There was that, and then there was another: a portrait I remember well. A bespectacled and biretted priest, his face of pale and pallid hue, eyes downcast (custody of the eyes and all that), hung, it was said, on the specific instructions of Arthur Couratin in a north light only to heighten the supposed ascetic effect – an image and sign for all to see on the staircase of Number 17 of the exemplar priest – a House-trained priest – one whose manner and mode was to be imitated by every student.

Ministry these days is not only a very worn word, it's a very mushy word, so you could well be forgiven for asking the question: Where has priesthood gone? Do we still in this Church of England believe in it? Are we still committed to it? For, increasingly, there is talk of ministry and ministerial and minister; little is heard of priest and priesthood of the priestly and the priest-like. So I should like to set before you some reflections on priesthood arising out of three particular feast days of this month: the Holy Cross; Hildegard of Bingen; and Charles Lowder. Each of these points us, I believe, to significant signs of the priestly character and life.

It is perhaps to state the obvious that the priest is first and foremost a sign of service – once a deacon always a deacon. Put more profoundly in that more modern poem/statement by William Vanstone which concludes his 'Love's Endeavour, Love's Expense', it is in Christ crucified that we discern the implications of what the priest as a sign of service must truly be 'Drained is love in making full; bound in setting others free; poor in making many rich; weak in giving power to be.' The holy cross is at the very heart of it all.

It is after the pattern of the Son of Man who came 'not to be served but to serve and to give his life as a ransom for many' that our priestly lives are to be fashioned. We are called to be servants of others, but even more challenging to be the slaves of God – *diaconia* and *doulos* are linked most effectively in that passage from Mark 10.43–5. Our slavery in that service to God is no burden. Rather it is in this service that we are to find our perfect freedom.

So those things for which this House is quite properly noted, and I hope continues so to be, are the priority for priesthood at all times and in all circumstances. It is the priority for prayer – that disciplined (because it will need to be that) steadfastness of adoration and praise and thanksgiving; of confession and intercession and anguished petition; of silence and solitude without which priesthood will lose its cutting edge and our priestly life descend into a kind of mindless activism which as one writer suggests, quite rightly I believe, becomes

> the more frenetic as the direction of the ministry becomes the more uncertain and which reduces the Church to a comfortable rotarianism where grace is hustled at bargain prices, only to replace the pursuit of holiness with a pursuit of narrow political, social or psychological goals.

The paradox is, of course, that it is precisely in your prayer that you serve your people best, being as one of my great predecessors, Archbishop Michael Ramsey, puts it 'before God with the people in your heart – being with Him for them and with them for Him'. Such is the nature of our priestly service. Hildegard of Bingen, known as the Sybil of the Rhine though perhaps rather better known in the popular mind as the singing nun of the twelfth century, reminds us of that holiness of life to which we are all called – the priest in particular – the priest as a sign of sanctity. She was not a particularly easy person to live with, but then whoever is? At times downright obstinate and objectionable yet even out of these 'weaknesses' God's amazing grace triumphs to bring forth her greatest strengths.

I am reminded again of Michael Ramsey whose biography by Owen Chadwick I have just been re-reading. Here was someone whose eyebrow movements became the more uncontrolled the more he became excited – as indeed did the number of his yeses – who could be seen at the early morning service with his braces hanging down the back of his vestment often the wrong way on a clown, a fool, well, yes, if you like – but for God's sake. His humanness was his holiness. I rather suspect he would never have made it these days through the selection processes!

The priest as a sign of sanctity, of holiness, speaks to us of the wholeness and wholesomeness of our lives, that they are as the Ordinal puts it 'framed and fashioned according to the Doctrine of Christ'; that there should be a consonance between the public and the private, above all that we should be ourselves, our own God-given character and characteristics fulfilled in His service.

Hildegard, as with so many of the saints, is an encouragement to us that we should not give up on ourselves, for God never does. Rather, in those moments of our greatest lostness and God-forsakenness he is there bearing with us, holding, giving, loving. The signs of our sanctity are not to be found in the sanctuary, rather they will be evidenced in the way in which we treat one with another and not least where there are sharp differences of view, strong and acute feelings on one side or the other on a particular issue or subject, controversial matters which constantly threaten to divide and yet where we are all called to strive fervently for that unity of the spirit in the bond of peace. For what hope is there for so many out there who are seeking, searching, surfing, if the Church is so wholly consumed with its own internal agendas? It is St Hildegard who points the way when she writes:

> People retain a glimmering of their knowledge of God. They should allow God to return to the centre of their lives, recognising that they owe their very existence to no one else save God alone, who is the creator of all.

So the question for us at the start of this twenty-first century is how is it possible to allow God to return to the centre of people's lives, beginning of course with ourselves and our churches? Does the worship, the prayer, the life of our Church and congregation in all its aspects enable people to apprehend something of the beauty, the splendour, the glory, the love of God, or is it all but some pale reflection of our own supposedly well-devised policies and strategies?

It is perhaps surprising, given the opposition he endured from the Church of England, that one hundred years or so ago later the very same church should include his name as one worthy of commemoration. I speak of course of Charles Lowder, one of those 'Reverend Rebels' as Bernard Palmer calls them. And with his name I link my final sign of priesthood: the priest as a sign of sacrifice, the priest as martyr, as witness in living and in dying to the sacrificial love of Christ given once and for all on Calvary's tree and proclaimed here anew this day in these holy and sacred mysteries. Certainly he was caught up in and savaged by what is termed the ritualist controversy. But the candles on the Holy Table, the vestments, the incense, 'the bells and smells' dimension of the Catholic movement were never ends in themselves. They were but the means of drawing souls closer to God – a way of engaging every part of the human person into the highest form of activity the human person can perform namely, the worship of God.

The sanctuary became the springboard for mission, for it was here in the offering of this Holy Sacrifice that the sacrifice of Christ's own self-offering was then to be lived out in the highways and the byways, among the downcast and the downtrodden, the needy and the poor, the sick and the dying of his parish. Where is that spirit of sacrifice today? Not a miserly begrudging and negative attitude to that which has been entrusted to us – namely, a share in the high priesthood of Christ – but rather a generous and joyful engagement with God's people whatever the situation, whatever the circum-stances. It is that ready and willing response, day by day, to that Charge in the Ordinal: 'Serve them with joy, build them up in faith, and do all in your power to bring them to loving obedience to Christ.' It was when he was addressing his parish following one of the most wounding and wicked attacks that Lowder told them 'The purpose of this address is to impress upon you the great beauty of showing by your lives that you really value these church privileges. That is after all the best answer to these attacks – the witness of our lives and those of our people.'

So then I leave you with these reflections: the priest as a sign of service, as a sign of sanctity, as a sign of sacrifice. They are not particularly popular qualities in an age which seems to count success only in terms of numbers, rising markets, greater financial rewards and so on. Above all, our business, like that of our blessed patron Stephen, is to keep our eyes fixed firmly on God, on His will and His way for us and for our Church, that we may be drawn more completely and more fully into the perfection of His love and the beauty of His holiness, and in being so drawn draw many others into that same unending love, the profligacy of the divine love given here so generously in this bread of life and the cup of the New Covenant.

So we have come – and so we go rejoicing and confident that He who has called us and given us a share in this priesthood of service, sanctity and sacrifice is faithful, and will be so, faithful to the end of our days.

Twenty

Decade of Evangelism Consultation – House of the Resurrection, Mirfield

Tuesday, 12 September 2000

'Go therefore and make disciples of all nations' (Matthew 28.19)

It was the Lambeth Conference in 1988 which for the Anglican Communion launched the Decade of Evangelism. There were two resolutions: the one spoke of evangelism as 'the primary task given to the Church', and every province of the Communion, in co-operation with other Churches, were encouraged to make 'the closing years of this millennium a Decade of Evangelism with a renewed and united emphasis on making Christ known to the people of His world'. The second resolution, following, called for what it described as a 'shift' throughout the Church world-wide to a dynamic missionary emphasis going beyond care and nurture to proclamation and service. And here was a call in 1988 which was not confined to the Anglican Communion alone. You may well recall that around the same time the Pope called for a similar renewed initiative in evangelization, and talked about a 'birthday present' for Christ at the dawn of a new millennium. Similarly, in other Churches and in other nations world-wide it seemed as if there was an almost unsought for yet spontaneous movement of the Holy Spirit urging the Churches to take new initiatives for evangelization.

Ten years or so down the line, what has been the result of these initiatives? The cynic might well argue nothing much. In fact, perhaps things have got rather worse than better, at least judging from the results of those regularly published church attendance figures where for pretty well every 'institutional' Church in this land, and generally in the Western world, the downward spiral has continued to the extent that many are asking 'Where will it all end?' That, I believe, would be a very particular and very negative interpretation of the facts. And in any case, the point might well be made that things might have been even bleaker had not the evangelistic initiatives, many and varied, been taken by the Churches. Even Peter Brierley in his *The Tide is Running Out* is not entirely and hopelessly pessimistic, but he does, I believe, set before us some very relevant material and pertinent questions to which we would do well to attend.

Well, it could be argued that that is precisely what the Christian Church/Churches have done over the centuries and sometimes with some pretty disastrous results. Evangelism, if it is anything, can never be simply coercion, about compelling them to come in, and in to what it might be asked? Are we just about – to use that rather vulgar phrase – bums on pews, or are we about the transformation of lives, along with the Saviour proclaiming the Good News of God's kingdom come on earth as it is in heaven? Or are we altogether caught up in, bound up with, weighed down by, the very institutions we seek to sustain?

There have been two very significant 'evangelistic' events this year – though neither of these would I suspect identify themselves at all as such – from which lessons might be learnt. The one earlier in the year was the exhibition at the National Gallery, 'Seeing Salvation'. Not a sermon preached, not a consultation held, not a word spoken. But they came in their thousands: believer and non-believer, seeker and searcher and surfer, agnostic and atheist. They 'saw' salvation! And note the emphasis on the 'seeing', the 'beholding'. As Churches we certainly need to become less wordy. We are in danger of becoming very chatty Churches. We need to encourage this altogether deeper and more profound apprehension in people in beholding the splendour, the beauty, the glory of God, the contemplative dimension.

The other not altogether dissimilar event was the mysteries of our salvation as they were presented in York Minster. For some twenty-five nights and with tickets sold at one thousand per night hardly had the Mystery Plays opened than the tickets were sold out. And almost to a person those coming away from the 'performance' – young and old, all manner of people – were making comments such as 'My life will never be the same again', 'That really has spoken to me tonight', 'I am going to have to think further about all this'. How many, I wonder, leave the worship of our churches with such comments and questions? What can we learn which is of real significance for evangelization from these two events? They certainly seem to have touched on those deep-down things – the spiritual – which that survey on the Soul of Britain revealed to be of primary concern for many people.

The Tablet commented:

> People believe in and are discovering a spiritual side to their lives, so much that they declare prayer to be the most important of all their spiritual experiences ... for church goers, spirituality and religiosity are closely related, but outside this group there is little overlap between the two, reinforcing the view that when people declare they are spiritual they are not declaring themselves to be religious ... the nation is seeking spiritual guidance and the churches are not seen to be providing it.

One might add perhaps 'Seeing Salvation' and the Mystery Plays are!

I hardly ever hear these words without my mind invariably turning to a small book which I bought when I was at Nottingham University – one of those SCM paperbacks at 7s. 6d. by Bishop Lesslie Newbigin, *Honest Religion for Secular Man* – a very politically incorrect title these days! In the chapter on 'Being God's People' (note again the 'being') he makes the point?

> The Church like the Israel of old has listened to those words 'Come unto me' but not listened to the words 'Go and I am with you'. It has understood itself more as an institution

than an exhibition. Its typical shape in the eyes of its own members, as well as of those outside, has not been a band of pilgrims who have heard the word 'go', but a large and solid building which, at its best, can only say 'come', and at its worst says, all too clearly, 'stay away'.

Evangelism, if it is about anything at all, must surely be about engagement – engagement with God, engagement with others, engagement with the Church itself, more in the sense of 'being with' than 'doing to'. Again, this is one of the reflections which Peter Brierley offers – 'encouraging church people to build real friendships with non-church people – not just an open door but an open heart'. Such an approach, too, would garner those beholding and seeing words – the Church as exhibition rather than institution – helping people 'behold' the presence of the living God in every part of their lives. Perhaps, in the end, it means that we are being led to discern quite new and different ways of being Church, where those models of institution and hierarchy have to be replaced with altogether simpler and less static images. The Church as *koinonia*, where relationship/community are so vitally important; the Church as pilgrim, a people on the way, ready to travel light; the Church as herald, a Church joyful and confident in its risen and ascended Lord – not boastful or arrogant or rude – but a Church in which that self-giving love given once and for all on Calvary's tree and proclaimed here in these holy and saving mysteries in which we behold all the riches of the divine grace so freely and so generously given here surely is the beginning and end of all mission – in that while we were yet sinners Christ died for us – God sent His only begotten Son – so that all may have life – life in all its abundance – the riches of His divine life for all.

And that must surely be why we cannot give up or give in, not because of our own intransigence or obstinacy or pride but rather because of that commission given by the risen Lord to those first disciples. The same Lord this and every day commissions you and me and every Christian person – 'Go ... and make disciples ... and above all and know that I am with you always – yes to the end of time.'

Twenty One

St Salvador's Church, Dundee

Holy Cross Day, Thursday, 14 September 2000

'Let this mind be in you which was also in Christ Jesus' (Philippians 2.5)

Over the last month or so, whilst taking my summer break – as I always have for the last twenty-five years – in the north-west highlands of Scotland, I have been dipping again into the book by Bernard Palmer, a former editor of the *Church Times: Reverend Rebels*. The title says it all! It is a fascinating and lively study of five Victorian clerics and the stand they took against authority, both civil and ecclesiastical. It was the second wave of the Oxford Movement when arguments raged around vestments and ornaments and forms of service, about what nowadays tends to be called the 'bells and smells' aspects of worship. At the end you are left wondering where does all that leave us today, what was their achievement? Has it any continuing relevance or value? Or are they and all that they stood for now simply to be consigned to a passing phase in the history of our Church, for which we must be profoundly thankful, but from which now we need to be moving on to other and more exciting challenges and possibilities?

Today, on this feast of the Holy Cross, we celebrate the one hundred and twenty-sixth anniversary of the consecration of this church. It is a considerable privilege and pleasure to be with you all for this your Patronal Festival. And what a magnificent building you have! As I entered I was at once taken back to the very beginning of my own ministry in Liverpool – to St John's Church, Tuebrook, in Liverpool, a church planned and designed by the very same architect, G. F. Bodley, and with such remarkable similarities. The day had been set for the opening and consecration of that church, but it was not to be. The arrangements had to be abandoned. Bodley's reredos, very similar to this, had to be removed before the then Bishop of Liverpool would agree to its opening. It was allegedly altogether too Romish and Popish – in fact not half so Romish and Popish that the church came to be once opened – to the extent that it fell under the ban, paradoxically only to flourish the more, and when, for example, confirmations were needed, the next time a returning colonial Bishop was passing nearby he was hauled in for the occasion! Perhaps the flying bishop concept is not quite so novel after all! There was much knock-about and banter and baiting on both sides – a good deal of it, sadly at times, ill-tempered and inappropriately confrontational too – there are surely important lessons from those times still to be learned today.

So as we give thanks for the past in this present and on this day, what is it to which we need to be attentive for the future? After all, we are the inheritors of a movement in the Church which stimulated deep learning and scholarship, which saw the Christian faith taught and preached in a vigorous and uncompromisingly evangelistic fashion, and above all else which was dominated by a fiery enthusiasm for mission: that, to quote the Book of Common Prayer, 'God's children who are in the midst of this naughty world might be saved through Christ for ever'. Even their detractors and persecutors admired them – these 'Reverend Rebels' – for their passionate zeal to save souls.

As then we look forward and we look ahead, what is your agenda to be? I would suggest for reflection this evening three areas which may conveniently be termed perseverance in prayer; care for the community; energy for evangelism.

At the heart of the Tractarian revival there was the centrality of this sacrifice of praise, the Eucharist, with the desire for the worshipping of God in the beauty of holiness. Those early struggles about the wearing of vestments, the use of candles on the Holy Table, the reservation and adoration of the Sacrament, were never intended to become struggles simply about the sanctuary and its ornamentation. Rather these were the very means, the outward and visible signs and symbols of the inwardness of these holy and awesome mysteries – the means whereby the worshipper would indeed be enabled through God's amazing grace and mercy to put on that servant, self-emptying mind of Christ, to enter more deeply and more fully into the mystery of God's love displayed supremely in the holy cross. The sacrificial aspect of the Eucharist was reflected in sacrificial living – a simplicity of life, a rule of life, lives lived out of love for God and others. We certainly need to recover that perseverance in prayer out of which sprang much which was so attractive and compelling.

There is a need at the beginning of this third millennium for a new asceticism. The Lambeth Conference 1998 described it as 'a theology of enoughness', where we shall make a clear priority in our busyness and noisiness for prayer, for space and silence and stillness; for being present at this Holy Eucharist; for the reflective study of the Holy Scriptures; for seeking the sacrament of forgiveness and reconciliation – in other words, all that which is the very stuff of Christian living – that which is described as 'holiness of life'. And it is no use talking about it, reading about it, even sharing about it – we actually need to get down on our knees and do something about it. In brief, in the words of the New Testament 'watch and pray'.

Perhaps one of the most significant and important achievements of the Oxford Movement was the clear emphasis it placed upon the ordained priesthood. It was not, however, a priesthood for the sanctuary but rather a priesthood for the people and with the people, especially a priesthood for the poor. The social dimension of the Gospel was at the very heart of what so many of those 'Reverend Rebels' were about. This is the context: urban priority, not only for this parish but for so many of those of the Tractarian tradition. Indeed, priests and people together have often been the trail-blazers for a social action which has developed and grown out of all proportion. I think, for example, of present-day housing associations, originating in the slum areas just north of King's Cross in London and at the initiative of priest and people together. This bias towards the poor has always been a key dimension of churches in this tradition and must continue so to be – these days not simply urban but also rural.

The transformation which is celebrated here in these sacramental mysteries is to be effected out there in the reality of people's lives and in the life of the world. Here is the foretaste – there is the action. So our horizons need to be wide and our vision very clearly outward looking. For no matter where you are there is that imperative towards active service – the servant Church as a model of the one who came not to be served but to serve – to give his life a ransom for many. It is St John Chrysostom who reminds us very powerfully that 'God has no need of golden vessels but of golden hearts ... adorn your temples if you will' ..., he writes, 'but do not forget your neighbour in distress – that person is a temple of infinitely greater value'. Care for community, then, is no mere slogan. It is at the very heart of God and should be equally so at the heart of the Church's life, that recognition of the dignity and worth of each and every human being, whoever they may be, whatever their colour, class or gender – they are to be supported, nourished, celebrated. Such is the inescapable consequence of Christ's own 'taking upon himself the form of a servant and being made in human likeness'.

Remember, too, you are members of an ecclesial community. How good it is to have Neville your bishop with us this evening. We have known each other for some forty years now and I personally have valued enormously our friendship over the years and in particular his generous welcome and hospitality to me in this diocese today. For whilst there may be differences and diversity of view on particular issues, that same respect, courtesy and hospitality is to be extended even in deepest disagreement – such is the nature of the mind of Christ: the readiness to hold fast the unity (community) which the spirit gives and alone can give in the bond of peace.

If perseverance in prayer and care for community are priorities for our agenda for the future, so, too, surely must be an energy for evangelization – that indefatigable and indomitable zeal for the winning of souls for Christ. It was not only the great priestly names, the 'Reverend Rebels', it was as much the contribution of the laity which drew so many women and men to a love for the Lord Jesus Christ and a deeper care and concern for each other. The energy for evangelization, for that going out and loving and serving the Lord in His world, is the responsibility of each and every one of us. How right that great missionary bishop Lesslie Newbigin was when he wrote that the Church has listened far too much to the Saviour's words 'Come unto me', whilst it has hardly listened at all to the command 'Go and I am with you.' Each of us is an ambassador for Christ, day by day, hour by hour, wherever we may be, whatever the situation and circumstance and it will not so much be by what we say or indeed by the measure of our religiosity or churchiness – rather in our being and by our doing that our mission will be the more effective. Remember it was St Francis of Assisi who said 'Go and preach the Gospel . . . but with words if you must!' How I wish my Church would heed that advice the more.

On this day, then, as we give thanks for this house of prayer, for this place which is none other than the gate of heaven, we are drawn into the transforming power of the Holy Spirit. We join with angels and archangels and with the whole company of heaven as on the distant ear we hear the endless song of heaven. We catch a glimpse of God's glory – we are fed with the bread of heaven and the cup of the New Covenant and, so refreshed and renewed, we are sent forth and sent out – as have so many in that long line of witnesses before us – to live and to love.

May each and every one of us, then, so follow in the way of Jesus Christ crucified and risen that many others may find it possible so to follow and come to find the same Jesus Christ to be for them their way, their truth, their life.

Twenty Two

Liturgical Conference, York University –

Eucharist – Friday, 22 September 2000

'This is how one should regard us, as servants of Christ and stewards of the mysteries of God' (1 Corinthians 4.1)

It is the common experience of those who, like myself, have a more roving commission, so to speak, when making enquiry of the local vicar about the liturgical use of the parish, that the response so often comes – with that slight air of astonishment that one should even have needed to ask the question in the first place – its just the usual service! My only reflection is: Well there are some pretty unusual 'usual services' around these days! In fact, I am often reminded of those skittish verses by S.J. Forrest which conclude

> Oh, just the usual thing, you know; but very up to date,
> Our basis is the liturgy of 1928,
> With lots of local colouring and topical appeal,
> And much lighthearted happiness, to make the service real;
> Our thoughts on high to sun and sky, to trees and birds and
>   rooks,
> Our altar nearly hidden in a library of books;
> The *Nunc Dimittis*, finally 'God Save The Queen' we sing;
> But apart from these exceptions, just the ordinary thing.

And, of course, there will be those who will argue that with the production of *Common Worship* with its myriad possibilities, not to mention these or other suitable words, confusion will be the more confounded!

Well, I very much hope it isn't, and that surely must be one of the reasons at least why you have been here in York for this consultation. Service books are all very well. Of course we need the texts, the prayers and the psalms, the readings and the responses and all the rest of it – the shape and the order – but as already we know from experience thus far, the printed book, the printed word will never in and of itself produce good liturgy – common worship. So the pastoral presentation of these services is vital. Indeed, the publication of *Common Worship* at Advent this year is a very real opportunity for the whole Church of England – every priest every parish and every person – to reflect anew on that which is the heart beat of the Church's life: our common prayer and worship.

It is interesting that Paul does not here use the word *diakonos*, which is translated 'servant', but rather a word which describes a rower on the lower deck of a trireme – one of a number of slaves who rowed the oars, all pulling in the same direction – they had after all little choice in the matter! The point, of course, is that we are the servants of Christ; not only that, we are the stewards, guardians, safe-keepers, of the mysteries of God, and not least I would suggest in this matter of the liturgy and worship of our Church – servants – all hopefully pulling in the same direction; stewards – all mindful of the sacredness of that which has been entrusted to us. Worship is not and cannot be either the exclusive preserve of the ordained person, though undoubtedly that person, among others, has particular and special responsibilities within the worshipping life of the Church. Worship is the work of the whole people of God. And its direction must surely always be godward.

Of course, worship needs to be accessible, but it must not be accessible surely at the expense of its awesomeness. Both these words, 'accessible' and 'awesome', are to be held together in that which, week by week, together we do in Christ's name and to God's praise and glory. It is the experience of presence and participation – both God's and ours – in the power of the Holy Spirit through Jesus Christ our Lord. Presence and participation for transformation.

115

That opening dialogue at the beginning of the Eucharistic Prayer deliberately builds up a climactic introduction to the prayer itself. The exchange between president and people reminds the worshippers that they stand at the very threshold of heaven. The response to the invitation 'Lift up your hearts' is properly translated 'Already we have them with the Lord'. And what other consequence can there be, having hearts and minds and lives and souls so lifted up, than thanksgiving and adoration and praise to the God who has created all things and in Christ redeemed the world and its peoples? Here, indeed, are mysteries beyond telling, the wonderful works of God rehearsed before us and into which we ourselves through the power of the Holy Spirit are caught up as with angels and archangels and the whole company of heaven we sing the thrice holy song of the blessed.

The high point of this Eucharist is both Word and Sacrament – hence their fundamental unity. It is the Mount of Transfiguration when Peter, James and John not only hear the divine Word, they also behold the divine presence, the glory, the splendour, the beauty of God. No wonder their spontaneous reaction is 'Lord it is good to be here.' And how reluctant they are to let go and leave. The mood is caught so very well by that modern song/hymn: 'Be still for the presence of the Lord is moving in this place'. I just wonder how many of us on leaving Sunday morning worship can really hand on hearts say, 'Lord it is good to have been here', or do we rather not leave with a huge sigh of relief!

Of course we all have our own ideas about worship; what should be done, how it should be conducted. And there are immense and varied resources for worship available to us, perhaps as never before. The point is, though, that what might be appropriate and possible in a cathedral is surely not so in a rural or urban parish, and vice versa. Indeed, my experience is that every place is different – the building for a start – its shape and size and design. That will necessarily impose certain limitations. It will also offer some possibilities, however modest and apparently unpromising. I have experienced the most effective and moving worship in the smallest and remotest of rural churches, but with the imaginative use of such very limited resources as were available to them and in a building which offered little in the way of movement. However, with Readers who read with prayerful attentiveness to the text; with intercessions by a farmer's wife which were prayed in anguish of heart, certainly very much on behalf of the local congregation and community and yet with an eye open to the needs of others and a succinctness which was commendable; and instead of struggling through the *Magnificat* and *Nunc dimittis* to Anglican chant which I had done the previous week and with such depressing results – these Canticles said prayerfully in the context of a haunting introduction and conclusion by a gifted flautist in the village, made for worship which was as simple as it was direct, accessible as it was profound and deeply moving – awesome. Yes, it was certainly good to have been there. No doubt all of you will have similar experiences to recall and recount.

Again, hopefully, this consultation and others like it around the dioceses will enable us all to listen and to share, to hear the experience of others in worship and to share best practice. The best practice of all, of course, is where the worship has been prayerfully prepared by priest and people together, and not with every one attempting to do everything – remember participation is often most effective simply in being there.

There remains much to be done throughout our Church as we prepare for and move towards the introduction of *Common Worship*. Hopefully this consultation will have served not only to instruct and inform but also to encourage and energize us now to take into the dioceses those good things which we have both heard and experienced. For if indeed we are servants of Christ and stewards of the mysteries of God, then there cannot surely be anything more vital and important as that time and that place in which 'we assemble and meet together to render thanks for the great benefits we have received at God's hands, to set forth his most worthy praise, to hear his most holy Word, and to ask those things which are requisite and necessary, as well for the body as the soul'. In short, the common worship of the whole people of God.

Twenty Three

Installation of Martyn Jarrett as Suffragan Bishop of Beverley and the inauguration of his ministry as Provincial Episcopal Visitor for the Province of York

York Minister – Saturday, 7 October, 2000

'Jesus said: "I am the good shepherd, the good shepherd lays down his life for the sheep"' (John 10.11)

The announcement of an appointment to an episcopal office or see, in addition to everything else, usually brings with it a veritable flood of complimentary, even adulatory, letters. It is recorded in his diary that a predecessor of mine, William Magee, then Dean of Cork, on receiving so large and unsolicited a variety of letters, wrote to a friend and colleague as follows:

> They are a curious miscellaneous collection; five from clerical tailors, who offer me all possible garments; two from photographers who want my face; two from clergymen

who want my 'countenance' in the Diocese; one writes to ask for my Chaplaincy, 'or any other post', on the strength of having known me briefly at University. Another writes congratulations, and gets his wife and mother-in-law to write separate letters, asking for a parish for him

And so he goes on! And such is the experience of us all, and not least, I suspect, yourself, Martyn. And in view of the particular dimension of the episcopal office and ministry to which today we commission you, there are and there will be varied and huge expectations.

If, by chance, you should be looking for a job description you will find none better than those opening verses of Ephesians 4. And not only yourself as a bishop in the Church of God, but each and every one of us entrusted with the 'shepherding' of the flock of Christ – 'Be humble always and gentle … patient too … putting up with one another's failings … spare no effort to make fast with bonds of peace the unity which the spirit gives.'

The bishop's commission is both pastoral and evangelistic; and it is expressed chiefly I would suggest through the ministry of presence and encouragement – your presence and your encouragement with and among those to whom you are shepherd, both as suffragan bishop of this Diocese of York and as Provincial Episcopal Visitor for this Northern Province. You are to be a shepherd to the shepherds – a servant to the servants, yes, even a slave – not to the desk and endless committees and administration and the impossible amounts of paper which increasingly descend upon us; nor for that matter to those impossible expectations which both clergy and people alike will have of you as a sort of sanctified Mr Fixit. Rather as a good shepherd you are bound both to priests and people – to build them up in the faith of the apostles; to encourage them in their fight against the world, the flesh and the devil; to give them all joy in believing as they seek to live Christ's risen life amidst the confusions, anxieties and complexities of our present age.

No one can pretend that the move from Burnley to Beverley is likely either to be easy or straightforward. There are differences, tensions and disputes within the Church itself;

there is confrontation, hatred and violence in the world, some of it generated by long-standing religious animosities. To you, Martyn, is given a special commission this day as Provincial Episcopal Visitor for this Northern Province. It is the ministry of pontifex: not to lord it over others in the grand manner you may be expected to do now and again, but to be a true pontifex – a bridge builder – to keep open the lines of communication with and between those who find themselves in profound disagreement, not least on the particular matter of the ordination of women to the ministerial priesthood – to assist us all not to pit ourselves over and against each other – and that goes for all of us – but rather always to seek to live in the highest possible degree of communion one with another, not only for our own and the Church's well-being, but for the sake of the world. This, I believe, is the core of that spokesman and adviser role to which reference is specially made in the Act of Synod and the context of the extended episcopal ministry which you are to exercise among us. Hear well the words of one of our episcopal colleagues from another Communion –

The Bishop discharges his task of preserving the unity of the Church, if he knows how to be a home from home for everybody and how to be at home with everyone. Thus the unity of the Church is determined less by doctrine than the way Christian people treat each other

– and not just the unity of the Church either, but the unity of neighbourhoods, communities and nations.

However strong our beliefs and principles may be, there must always be among us those overarching Christian virtues of respect, patience, courtesy and charity. It is on these that all of us stand under judgement. So whilst we cannot be deaf to current divisive issues or to new threats either within the Church or in society and the world, we can and we must continue to take to heart those opening words of chapter four of Paul's Letter to the Ephesians – ever striving to hold fast and build up yet further the bonds of mutual understanding, of reconciliation, pardon and peace; to be fervent in prayer for each other and not least those with whom we most disagree; and in all of this rejoicing in our common baptism into the death and resurrection of the one Lord and Saviour Jesus Christ who has called us into His service and entrusted us with a share in his high priesthood – that priesthood which bears the scars of the nails and which can only be exercised in the costliness of sacrificial self-offering.

We are not called either, as bishops, to some lowest common denominator kind of collegiality (not that I suspect for one moment, Martyn, that you are that kind of person anyway!). Rather we are called to be faithful first to the Lord of the Church and then through the gift of His spirit to each other – and note that this unity is gift and promise and not right or possession of any one exclusive group – that we all may be one that the world may believe. And this is precisely the point of it all: the world for which Christ died, that we shall not so much ourselves become captive to that spirit of divisiveness and contentiousness and conflict, but seek for ourselves, the Church and the world that transformation which is at the very heart of these holy and awesome mysteries: a transformation born of sheer generosity – the generosity of self-sacrificial love – the love which bears all things, hopes all things, endures all things. In short, God's eternal and everlasting love given us in Christ crucified and in which, in spite of all our diversity, all our differences, through the gift of His amazing grace alone we are one.

You will need to beware, Martyn, lest in preaching to others you also become a castaway. In other words you will need to guard your own inner life, to take heed to yourself, especially when there is so much and so many clamouring endlessly, ceaselessly for your attention, your support, your care, your time. For whatever else the bishop may or may not be – pastor, priest, prophet, evangelist, enabler and all the rest of those things we are told we are or should be – always remember first and foremost you yourself are a disciple of Jesus Christ – yourself a follower, a pilgrim on the way together with the rest of our Christian brothers and sisters in the Church of God and throughout the world. Thus Bishop Lesslie Newbigin aptly reminds us that 'the Bishop is not so much facing towards the Church as facing toward the Lord ... his ministry is so to follow Jesus in the way of the cross, that others find it possible to follow too'.

121

So now, in union with the Church throughout the world and down the ages, with saints in heaven and saints on earth, we pray fervently for you, Martyn, for the grace and power of the Holy Spirit upon you, with you and within you to strengthen and support, to guide and direct you in your ministry as Suffragan Bishop of this Diocese of York and Provincial Episcopal Visitor for this Northern Province; that entrusting you with this ministry, which is of such great excellency as well as so great difficulty, we pledge our continuing prayer and support for you, with you and alongside you.

It was the great Bishop Augustine who, long ago now, caught so exactly and so succinctly the work of a bishop

> to rebuke agitators, to comfort the faint-hearted, to take care of the weak, to take heed of snares, to teach the uneducated, to waken the sluggish, to hold back the quarrelsome, to put the conceited in their place, to appease the militant, to give help to the poor, to liberate the oppressed, to encourage the good, to endure the evil, and – oh – to love them all.

Yes, it is an impossible task – totally impossible in and of your own strength, but with God nothing is impossible. To the same God, then, be all might, majesty, dominion and power now and to the end of the ages. Amen.

Twenty Four

Dewsbury Minister – Day of Pilgrimage

Sunday, 8 October 2000

'There is one body and one Spirit ... one Lord, one faith, one baptism, one God and Father of us all, who is above all and through all and in all' (Ephesians 4.4–6)

If I were to set before you all that quiz–type question – 'What is it which brings together Bradford, Wakefield, Dewsbury and the Archbishop of York?' I rather suspect there could be the possibility of what is described as a multi-choice response. Commonalities of various types could be suggested, not least the fact that they all hail from God's own country – Yorkshire through and through – what more could you want or desire? It is not, however, our Yorkshireness, if I may so describe it, which has inspired this pilgrimage today. It is something, someone, altogether more fundamental than that. For the one person whom we all have in common – some more directly it has to be said than others – is Paulinus, and even more fundamentally still, the one Lord and Saviour Jesus Christ in the power of whose spirit we gather here in this Minister church. And if you want a display of that 'oneness' which Paul is so at pains to stress in the opening verses of chapter four of his letter to the Ephesians, here it is – here we are – disparate and diverse in a whole range of ways, yet together in pilgrimage, one in our journey of faith, one in our celebration of our common heritage; in short, one in Christ.

I am of course aware of those rather more mundane and

mercenary attachments which are alleged between Dewsbury, Wakefield and Bradford; namely, the payment of dues and tithes here to the church in Dewsbury, as signs of Dewsbury's claims to prominence and supremacy over the other two. Bradford; I believe, continue to pay their 40p per year. Wakefield gave up long ago – though it has to be said, by one born and bred in Wakefield, that, in Wakefield's defence, the revered John Walker in his history of the cathedral church of Wakefield notes that the only entry among a list of expenses of the Proctor of Dewsbury church is in 1349: 'Hire of a certain pasture for lambs coming of tithe of Dewsbury and Wakefield, 4s.' So whilst there may be pretty flimsy evidence for Dewsbury's claims over Wakefield, nevertheless the connection is plainly attested and Wakefield is surely glad to be associated with this 'gathering in of the fragments' today.

The focus of our celebration today, as already I have hinted, is Paulinus – a person of pilgrimage, a person of presence, and a person of proclamation. And it is on these three themes that I should like to suggest some reflections this afternoon. Paulinus was certainly a person of pilgrimage – pilgrimage was, after all, a quite natural dimension of mission. He was part of that second wave of missionary endeavour stemming from Gregory the Great who first sent Augustine to these shores and established a firm stronghold in the south of England. Paulinus' mission was directed very firmly to the heathen north. Here was one who like Abraham of old was prepared to forsake all that was familiar to him in order to go out, go forth, not knowing where he was to go. The missive from Gregory to Augustine was that Paulinus should establish York as a metropolitan see with twelve suffragans. Bede tells in vivid detail of the dramatic conversion and baptism of Edwin, King of Northumbria. It was a momentous breakthrough for the kingdom of God: but not content only with that, and given the huge size of Edwin's territory, Paulinus – as with so many of those earliest saints – went from place to place preaching the Gospel and baptizing people into this new and living way: the way of Jesus Christ who is the way, the truth and the life. Here was one who spent his whole life in gathering people not to himself but to Christ, a challenge to us all today, and where the pilgrim Church needs to become more of a reality; a style and model very relevant for the twenty-first century just as it was in the seventh.

Paulinus was a person of presence in the sense that he was out and about, in and among where people actually are. That was the 'place' of his ministry. It was in his going out and his going forth that he was able to 'gather up the fragments'. Here again is a very appropriate challenge for the Church today. Often the built heritage is perceived only in terms of being a burden, and there is no doubt that our church buildings do make huge demands on us financially. Equally, it has to be said, they offer, with real imagination and vision, the possibility of communicating the grace and truth of the Gospel not only to a wide range of people, young and old, but also to large numbers of people.

Here in this Minster you have produced and presented the current Dewsbury Festival of Christian Music. Already you have had Yorkshire's answer to Jim Reeves, and Rick Wakeman is yet to come, and in between you have managed jazz and plainsong, brass and piano! Many possibilities there for the gathering in! I am aware, too, of the ways in which both Bradford and Wakefield have properly and closely engaged with the local neighbourhood and community and region, an engagement which is surely its own evangelization. It is not only buildings, though, but people – you and I – all of us coming together in pilgrimage and in prayer, celebrating together the blessings of belonging, but then ourselves going out and going forth to be the good news for which today we give thanks.

It was that great missionary bishop, Lesslie Newbigin, who wrote a long time ago now in a passage on *Being God's People*, that far too often we listen to the Lord's words – 'Come unto to me' but fail equally to listen to his commission 'Go and I am with you.' He writes:

> The Church in the New Testament is portrayed as a body of people chosen and sent ... the disciples are not portrayed as mystics seeking the true religion and finding it in Jesus. They are shown rather as people picked for an expedition ... a task-force rather than a study group of a holy club.

That same commission to which Paulinus so readily and resolutely responded is entrusted to each and every one of us today: to go out, to live and to be, to share and to care and in so doing be ourselves an epiphany, an exhibition of the God who is 'above all and through all and in all', whose presence we have in Jesus.

Paulinus was also a man of proclamation. Proclamation, like evangelization as engagement; engagement with others, engagement with the local village and community, engagement with rich people and influential people; engagement especially like the Lord he followed with poor people and with the outcasts and sinners. It is to that ministry of engagement that you and I are equally called today. Indeed that is what this Dewsbury Festival of Christian Music intended to do – as with so many and similar initiatives both in Wakefield and Bradford – the many and varied points of contact not only with our fellow Christian brothers and sisters, but also with those of other faiths and of no faith at all. For each and every one of us is created in the image and likeness of God, the God 'who is above all and through all and in all'.

It is a former Suffragan Bishop of this Diocese, John Finney, in a study on bringing people to faith, who makes the point that one of the most effective ways of so doing is through a personal engagement with others – personal relationships and personal invitations. Similarly, Peter Brierley, in response to his recent survey on churchgoing, makes the point that we should be more encouraging of church people to build up friendships with non-church people – an open heart not just an open door. Just think, if each and every one of you here made it your particular responsibility to bring one additional person to faith and to church in the next twelve months – the difference that could begin to make in the life of our churches, in the life of our communities, in the life of the nation as a whole. But then it is not only a matter of proclamation and evangelization and engagement by way of bringing people to church. It is an evangelization which sends us forth and sends us out like Paulinus whom we celebrate today: out – out there to engage with God's world and God's people, with the anxieties, the perplexities, the complexities of so many people – so many who we know from so many polls and surveys are looking, seeking, searching, questing, surfing on-line for they know not what – and to whom and with whom we should, I believe, be addressing ourselves in faith and hope. It will not be a proclamation or evangelization of assertion and arrogance, it will rather be in weakness and fear and much trembling – that weakness, though, which is stronger than human strength – the weakness of the crucified Christ who is the power of God to transform not only our lives but the life of the entire world.

The only reason, then, why we have come here together on our pilgrimage in honour and in celebration of Paulinus is that we should be sent out and sent forth to continue this same pilgrimage, a pilgrimage both of presence and of proclamation. You are that presence; you are that proclamation; wherever you may be at every moment in every circumstance. You are an ambassador of the God who is above all and through all and in all, yourself a sign of weakness and failure, yes, of course – to that extent a sign of the cross – but strengthened too in the power of the same Christ crucified and risen, a sign of triumph ourselves, our lives an evident demonstration of God's power in weakness of His abundant mercy and grace even in our failure.

So hear well those words today. Go ... go in peace and in joy. Go in the strength of Christ. And in your own faithful following of Him who is risen may many others come so to follow and find in Him, Jesus Christ – the one who is the same yesterday, today and for ever – their way, their truth and that fullness and abundance of life which Jesus Christ wills for you and for the peoples of the entire world.

Twenty Five

Commemoration of Richard Hooker

The Temple Church, London – Monday, 13 November 2000

'For the earth shall be filled with the knowledge of the glory of the Lord, as the waters cover the sea' (Habakkuk 2.14)

I cannot be sure whether it is by accident or design that I find myself here in this pulpit on the occasion of the commemoration of Richard Hooker, Master of The Temple for six years, who died four hundred years ago this month. It seems, however, entirely appropriate for an Archbishop of York, and not least one who succeeded in that office from the Bishopric of London, to stand before you this evening. For it is highly probable that it was the influence of Edwin Sandys, Archbishop of York, formerly Bishop of London, who happened to be dining at The Temple very shortly after the Mastership of The Temple had fallen vacant, which was a determining factor in the appointment of Richard Hooker as Master of The Temple in 1585.

Sandys' son, of the same name, Edwin, had become a pupil of Hooker. The Archbishop therefore knew at first hand not only the temper of the man but also the temper of his discourse and the profundity of his learning. Already in the bitter exchange between the then Dean of York, Matthew Hutton, a fierce and fanatical Puritan, and the Archbishop, Sandys, something of what was to face Hooker here at The Temple had already been rehearsed. It was a question about the origins of

Holy Order – 'Dost thou call me a Papist?', Sandys is reported to have bellowed at Hutton: 'If I be a Papist thou art a Puritan', as indeed he was. Today such an exchange seems hardly possible, yet in reality it was a struggle which struck at the very heart and being of the Church of England. And it is striking that almost without exception Hooker's writings are concerned with the nature of the Christian Church. He points us to the Church and through the Church to Christ. For him the life of the Church: its teaching of the faith and study of the Scriptures; its offering of prayer and worship; its sacraments of baptism and the Eucharist; its pastoral care and concern for all is the life of grace, a source of strength, guidance and goodness for Christians in every age.

The Church of England was no new invention. Whilst wholeheartedly sharing in the Reformation's rediscovery of the grace of God in Jesus Christ, Hooker vigorously promoted the Church of England's continuity with the Church of the Middle Ages and the early Fathers. He would certainly have approved the position clearly expressed at an earlier stage by John Jewel in his *Apologia*, a work which has been described as 'one of the earliest, if not the earliest, essay in Anglican self-understanding'. Jewel wrote: 'We have planted no new religion, but only have preserved the old that was undoubtedly founded and used by the apostles of Christ and other holy fathers of the primitive church.' He insisted that

> This lawful Reformation . . . is so far from taking from us the name or nature of true Catholics . . . or depriving us of the fellowship of the Apostolic Church or impairing the right faith, sacraments, priesthood and governance of the Catholic Church that it hath cleared and settled them on us.

It was, of course, Hooker's lot to have to face, Sunday by Sunday, here in this very church, the regular weekly onslaught by Travers against him. Hooker's patient and reasoned sermon in the morning became the stuff of Travers's rebuttal in the afternoon. As Thomas Fuller went on to comment in the next century 'The pulpit spake pure Canterbury in the morning and Geneva in the afternoon . . . the gravest Benchers were not more exact in taking instructions from their clients than in writing notes from the mouths of their Ministers.' Here was the best show in London. As a recent biographer of Hooker puts it

> Here at The Temple one could witness the great religious issues that divided the nation fought out in a public arena as two gladiators of equal strength did battle for the minds and hearts of an influential and sophisticated audience.

And there can be no doubt about it, his early years of academic life in Oxford and subsequently as Vicar of St Mary's, Drayton Beauchamp, prepared him well for such disputations, which tested to the full the breadth of his learning, the painstaking care with which he both marshalled his arguments and set forth his views. Any one of lesser mind or without Hooker's remarkable intellect could never have withstood the relentlessness of Travers's refutations or the ingeniousness of his arguments.

The remarkable thing about Hooker is the tone not only of his preaching but of his writing. For at a time of considerable passion and polemic, when disagreements were sharp and divisions only too evident, Hooker's writings were paradoxically all the more polemical and passionate precisely because of their air of moderation, calm reasonableness and unfeigned charity. Though the elevated tone of the argument helped disguise the fact, *Of the Laws of Ecclesiastical Polity* is a ruthlessly effective work, returning as it does to the very first principles of philosophy and theology. This is the source of Hooker's authority and his enduring value. His work is grounded in his understanding of law and of the role of human reason in interpreting law. He stands within the natural law tradition. He points us to the rich resources of that tradition for our own very different society and world.

The 'brave design', as it has been described of Hooker's 'Books of Polity', was, as Paget very aptly writes:

> to display the universal field of law; to show how by the will and providence of God the whole world and all the ways of men are included in that system, vast and manifold, whereby through diverse channels the authority and beneficence of law travels to the diverse fields of human life; and then to

claim for the legislative action of the Church its rightful place and its divine sanction within that sacred system which reaches from the throne of the most high to the least of the creatures he has made.

Law for Hooker is almost divine. It permeates the created universe and reflects the nature of God, for divine law is inscribed in the Scriptures yet needs to be interpreted by human reason. He operates with the late mediaeval distinction between two sources of knowledge for the earthly life of human kind: the light of nature and the light of revelation, both interpreted by reason. Nature follows its ordered course according to natural laws ordained by its creator. When these natural laws are recognized, interpreted and followed by humanity we have the law of reason. Though nature and reason cannot show us the way of salvation, they overlap with the revealed Scriptures. Scripture and nature are neither mutually exclusive nor fundamentally opposed – 'The Scripture is fraught even with the laws of nature.'

Except in its fundamental Gospel, Hooker believes the Bible not to be self-explanatory. It requires interpretation by means of reason. In defending himself against Travers's charge here at The Temple that he had introduced scholastic distinctions and rational subtleties into the exposition of Scripture, Hooker explained what he meant by reason. He certainly did not mean his own individual reasoning capacity. What he meant was 'True, sound, divine reason ... theological reason' which brings to light the true meaning of the 'darker places' of Scripture.

The sphere of reason is the world of law – that ordered world that derives from God whose being is a law unto his working. The vocation of reason – for that is what it is – is to bring human existence into conformity with the order and harmony of the nature of things: 'All good laws are the voices of right reason, which is the instrument where with God will have the world guided.'

Reason for Hooker is therefore not autonomous, individualistic, arrogant or secular; it is not even particularly critical. His concept of reason is almost the antithesis of that of the Enlightenment. Reason for Hooker is a divinely implanted faculty for apprehending the truth revealed by God in nature or

Scripture. It is first receptive, then discriminating. It seeks the good for humanity – 'Goodness is seen with the eye of the understanding and the light of that eye is reason.'

Hooker is unquestionably a reformed theologian with a strong sense of what the English Church owes to Luther and to Calvin but he has no time for the Puritans with their biblical absolutism or for the notion that the Church of England should shun anything used by the unreformed Church of Rome. Equally, he argues powerfully against the absolutism of the Roman Catholic position with its appeal to the infallibility of the Church and the Pope. He argues rather for a practical faith, insisting that the highest form of certainty we can enjoy is that of probable 'persuasions'. Though the human mind craves 'the most infallible certainty which the nature of things can yield', this craving cannot be satisfied. Assent to truth must always be proportionate to the evidence. Certain knowledge is not given to humanity in its earthly pilgrimage. Probability is our guide in this life. Hooker insisted on the totality of truth. We need Scripture and tradition interpreted by the collective wisdom of the Church through the ages. Reason is corporately exercised under the guidance of tradition which comprises the accumulated wisdom of the Church. His appeal to tradition is partly pragmatic, born of respect and prudence. 'Neither may we ... lightly esteem what hath been allowed as fit in the judgement of antiquity, and by the long continued practice of the whole Church; from which unnecessarily to swerve, experience hath never as yet found it safe.' Hooker's view of the way authority works has been described by R. W. Church as 'The concurrence and co-operation each in its due place of all possible means of knowledge for man's direction'. The spirit of Hooker's understanding of authority is therefore organic, communal, constitutional, judicious and balanced.

So, then, we may ask what is the Gospel according to Hooker? He does not provide a systematic account of basic Christian belief. This is not his purpose. But he was compelled to clarify his faith in his debate with Walter Travers, his colleague and rival here at The Temple Church. It is in this dispute with Travers that Hooker clarifies the essential Gospel. This for Hooker simply comprises the person and work of Jesus Christ. Again and again he returns to this with radical simplicity and evangelical passion. The foundation of the faith, the crucial thing in Christianity, is 'Christ crucified for the salvation of the world'; or again, 'salvation purchased by the death of Christ'. We could say, for Hooker Christianity is Christ.

In his fullest statement on this theme Hooker writes

> This then is the foundation where upon the frame of the Gospel is erected; that very Jesus whom the Virgin conceived of the Holy Ghost, whom Simeon embraced in his arms, whom Pilate condemned, whom the Jews crucified, whom the apostles preached, he is Christ the only Saviour of the world, other foundation no man can lay.

This 'precious' doctrine, this 'inestimable treasure', is the 'rock' which forms the foundation of the Church. The Church is the place where grace and nature, revelation and reason, Gospel and law meet and find their ultimate harmony in Jesus Christ. If Christianity is Christ it is also the Church of Christ. We cannot have the one without the other. Perhaps we should allow Hooker the final word:

> For his Church Christ knoweth and loveth so that they which are in the Church are thereby known to be in him ... we are therefore adopted sons of God to eternal life by participation of the only begotten son of God, whose life is the well-spring and cause of ours.

For the life, the witness and the writing of Richard Hooker, Master of The Temple 1585–91, we this night bless God's holy name, beseeching him to give us grace so to follow his good example that with him we may be partakers of God's heavenly kingdom.

To the same God then be all praise and thanksgiving now and to the end of the ages. Amen.

Twenty Six

Clergy Day

York Minster – Monday, 4 December 2000

'They who wait for the Lord shall renew their strength, they shall mount up with wings like eagles, they shall run and not be weary, they shall walk and not faint' (Isaiah 40.31)

Waiting is very much a fact of life. It always has been. It always will be. Whoever you are, wherever you are, waiting is part of the experience of being human. Even before each of us is born there is that nine month or so period of waiting, waiting to be born. People speak, too, of waiting to die. And in between, one way or another, there seems to be an awful lot of waiting: waiting it has to be said, for the most part, which is frustrating, annoying, disruptive, resented even angry waiting, as recent events on the railways have readily demonstrated. And then there is the less spectacular waiting which we accept very much as part of our everyday lives: at the bus stop, a queue at the supermarket check-out, for a friend to arrive, and so on. Again, there are those for whom there is no other option in life but waiting; refugees, displaced persons, the hungry, homeless people who have nothing else to do but to wait, with little prospect of much else for the future either, except more waiting.

In sharp contrast the prophet sets out here the altogether more positive outcome for those whose waiting is upon the Lord. Israel is in crisis – they have been taken into exile – their faith has been severely tested; that which was thought quite inconceivable for God's elect and chosen people, has happened – dereliction and destruction has come upon them, they have been removed even from the land promised to them and their offspring for ever. Dreams have been shattered, hopes have been dashed. Yet even in this darkest of times and circumstances a glimmer of light beams out. Deutero-Isaiah announces the imminence of salvation for the entire people of God. The fortieth chapter begins with those majestic and momentous words of comfort and consolation, of peace and of hope: 'Comfort, comfort my people, says your God ... Speak tenderly to Jerusalem ... the glory of the Lord shall be revealed and all flesh shall see it together.'

This is the context in which the strength of those who wait upon the Lord is to be renewed, the reason why they shall 'mount up with wings like eagles – run and not be weary, walk and not faint'. It is not by their own strength or power, their own resilience or might – exile has demonstrated to them just how utterly useless any such attempts in their own strength alone have been. Rather it is the Lord who is the everlasting God, the creator of the ends of the earth, the one who does not faint or grow weary, who is the source and wellspring of that life and liveliness to those who wait upon him. Further, here is a waiting which is very different both in nature and manner to much of our own experience of waiting. It is a waiting which is a longing – an expectant and hopeful waiting – an eager and excited waiting – a waiting in faith, by faith and through faith – most of all a waiting in the confidence of God.

With less than four weeks to go to Christmas this is probably not exactly the best time to be urging the virtues of patient and persistent waiting! Yet this in part is the inescapable message of this season of Advent. It is after all a waiting to celebrate – 'now in the time of this mortal life' – an event which is both past and future, the coming to us 'in great humility of our Saviour Jesus Christ', and that last day 'when he shall come again in his glorious majesty to judge both the living and the dead'. Both are awesome events, and our lives are lived in the in-between.

So what, then, of this 'waiting for the Lord' for those of us so busy seeking to respond as best we can to the seemingly ever-increasing demands and expectations of the ministry which has been entrusted to us? I should like to set before you all briefly this morning three areas for your further reflection on this text and what it might mean for you as an individual minister of the Lord, called, chosen and sent, and all of us together. Waiting as presence; waiting as prayer; waiting as protest.

You may not have heard the name Nicholas Herman, but you may just have heard of his more commonly known name, Brother Lawrence, the author of that spiritual classic, a collection of his conversations and letters, *The Practice of the Presence of God*. In his simple, unsophisticated and quite unselfconscious way he speaks and writes of that sense of God's presence each and every moment, not least in the most ordinary commonplace and mundane things. He is banished to the monastic kitchen, for which he has no training and found to be not at all to his liking – yet the paradox is that that is precisely the place where he discovers God's presence.

Here is a way of prayer which is a way of life; the Celtic tradition and indeed the Jewish prayer tradition are very similar in nature and in style. And it is a way of prayer which came very much alive for me some fifteen years or so ago now when first I visited Tanzania and accompanied the Bishop of Central Tanganyika. I remember at almost every stage, before setting out on a long journey – during the journey – on arrival – there was a pause and a prayer, a waiting upon the Lord, a waiting which is a presence, a pervading and pervasive presence – day by day, hour by hour, moment by moment – enfolded in the presence of God. Clearly linked with this waiting as presence is waiting as prayer. It was Desmond Tutu, you will recall, who made that astonishing statement that he was far too busy *not* to pray for two hours every day.

And any trawl through the witness of Anglican devotion produces a prodigious number of examples of prayerful devotion. Robert Bolton, for example, the Puritan incumbent of Broughton, Northamptonshire, in the early seventeenth century prayed six times a day: twice by himself, twice with his family, twice with his wife. That great evangelical preacher, Charles Simeon, rose, it is said, at 4.00 a.m. to give four hours to prayer and Bible study. William Grimshaw, a fiery and formidable Lancastrian pastor and preacher of the eighteenth century, wrote:

As soon as you awake in the morning employ an hour in five

things – bless God for the mercies of night past – praise him for a new day and pray for the blessing of it – examine well your own hearts – meditate upon some spiritual subject – and lastly plan out the business of the day.

One entry in his diary for 1756 reads: 'A day of net mending; no preaching – reading, meditation and prayer have been my chief exercise and Imployment.'

So, brothers and sisters, what about your days of net mending? I mention these examples not to make anyone feel guilty but rather to focus our hearts and minds on that passage in the Ordinal and the Ordination Service which reminds us all that 'because you cannot bear the weight of this ministry in your own strength but only by the grace and power of God, pray earnestly for His Holy Spirit.' Wait upon the Lord – wait upon Him with patience, with wonder and with love. It is he who alone can and will renew your strength.

Finally, there is waiting as protest. And it has to be surely slightly crazy, to say the least, when things are piling up, when the pressure is on, when expectations are increasing and responsibilities multiply and when busyness is at a premium – to be recommending the busyness of being rather than doing. It is the business of actually daring to take the risk of breaking the mould – the sheer drivenness of diary and of the day and of recognizing the need for some net mending – net mending godwards – but also for yourself and your family; yourself and your friends; the protest to be human which is a protest for the whole of humanity as much as it is for yourself – that there is a better way of life and living than simply being caught up ever more increasingly in the 'Tesco *ergo sum*' mentality! That after all was the protest of the early monastic movement into the Egyptian desert. It was the unfailing message of the northern saints: Cuthbert and Bede, Hilda and Aidan. Here was no self-indulgent spirituality but rather a clarion call to wake up to the truth of the Gospel, the reality of God and, above all else, the possibility in Jesus Christ for the transformation of life, the transformation of the Church, the transformation of the entire created order.

So, my brothers and sisters, seize the moment. Hear well the message of Advent as with eager expectation and watchful waiting upon the Lord each of us seeks to make attending to God a clear priority for ourselves, our congregations and our churches, for 'those who wait for the Lord shall renew their strength, they shall mount up with wings like eagles, they shall run and not be weary, they shall walk and not faint'.

Twenty Seven

Changing Church: Unchanging God

University of Cambridge – Sunday, 4 February 2001

'And he has put all things under his feet and has made him the head over all things for the church, which is his body, the fulness of him who fills all in all' (Ephesians 1.22,23)

There are but three mentions of 'church' in the Gospels, and all three exclusively within the Gospel of Matthew – a sharp contrast indeed to the volumes which have subsequently come to be written and the debate which continues on almost every aspect of what and how we are to understand in our use of the word 'church'. For the generality of people, your typical person on the Clapham omnibus, it's little more than a useful landmark by which to offer directions – turn right at the church in the centre of the village, on the corner of the street ... and so on. For such, it is no more than a building. For the insider who may have a rather deeper grasp of these matters 'church' is people and they may well argue that the building is more of a hindrance than it is a help in a better understanding of what Christian discipleship and Christian life is supposed to be about. Again the theologian may well have an entirely different perspective, raising questions about the *esse* of the Church, its being, its sacramentality, its essence, its purpose, its end, and so on.

I should like to address yet another dimension, not exclusive in and of itself, but which touches each of these albeit generalized statements. It is to do with models of the Church, and those models which I believe to be of particular relevance and value for the Church in the twenty-first century. There is, of course, in the New Testament as a whole – excluding the three references in the Gospel of Matthew – a considerable diversity and variety of images of the Church (the word has some one hundred or so mentions in all): true vine, bride of Christ, spiritual house, household of God, fullness of Christ, servant, and so on – and where already certain images are beginning to predominate, and not least the Pauline image of the Church as the Body of Christ and its extended outworking, for example in 1 Corinthians 12, and to which reference is crucially made in my text from Ephesians. However, before proceeding further it would perhaps be well to pause for a moment on the word *ecclesia* as it emerges in the New Testament itself. For here is a word which was quite secular in origin. It was never a 'church' word. As such it was deliberately chosen by the Septuagint translators to render the Hebrew *qahal Yahweh*. For they well knew the distinctiveness and uniqueness of this 'congregation of the Lord', and were at pains to ensure that it could never be represented by any word for a Greek religious society or pagan cult. Indeed, *ecclesia* is used in precisely this 'secular' sense in Acts 19.32.

As K. L. Schmidt points out in the *Theological Word Book of the New Testament*, the derivation of *ecclesia* is significant. It speaks to us of a gathering of people, an assembly, those who are the 'called out' ones, summoned by the herald (the one bringing the tidings: the news). Here is a people, then, with a vocation, a people primarily gathered before God to listen to Him, a people charged with a special responsibility before God for others. Incidentally, the New Testament, if it has any word at all for a 'place' of meeting for such an assembly, never uses *ecclesia* but, rather, *sunagoge*.

Clearly, the span of time from then to now has made for immense changes. From the Church in Corinth and Rome and Colossae and Philippi, *The Churches the Apostles Left Behind*, as one author describes them, to the institutional Churches of today with their committees and councils, their laws and legalities, their boards, their boundaries and their bureaucracies which seem to prompt in so many the somewhat wistful

140

and nostalgic view 'If only we could get back to the simplicity and straightforwardness of the Church of the New Testament.' Would that it were so simple and so straightforward!

So if I am to venture this morning some reflections on models of the Church for the twenty-first century just where are we to begin? I would suggest that we begin with a statement from the Greek Orthodox theologian John Zizioulas who, quite rightly I believe, gets to the heart of the matter when he writes:

> We cannot have an ecclesiology until we have a proper Trinitarian doctrine, for we cannot expect of the Church anything less than a sign and a reflection of God's way of being in creation ... the church must be conceived as the place where men (and women) can get a taste of their eternal eschatological destiny which is communion in God's very life.

What Zizioulas is saying in somewhat technical theological language is that if we are to begin to understand something of the character and being of the Church then we must necessarily begin first with the vision of God the Holy Trinity. And this surely must be the starting point for our own thoughts and reflections this morning. How, then, is it possible that the arcane mysteries of the Holy Trinity might assist us in a better understanding of who and what we are as Church?

The classical perception of God the Holy Trinity gives us some insight into God's way of being as that of Persons in relation, a relationship so profoundly reciprocal that they are one in being, so perfect in its mutuality that they will one will. The interaction in love of Father, Son and Holy Spirit is a depth of participation in one another which makes the Trinity a unity. From that life of mutuality and fellowship (*koinonia*) of the Godhead, love overflows into creation, sustaining the world in being and bringing it to its appointed end in glory. The gift of God to the Church is the privilege of sharing here and now in the divine life, and of extending that same love of God in the world. The Church's vocation, then, is to live and witness as a fellowship, a communion, a *koinonia*, which seeks to be one in its ecclesial being and one in its will to serve its Lord; and in a mutual love which gives individuals, and local communities, and diverse Christian traditions, scope fully to be themselves and to participate equally in the common life.

To stress that the Church is communal is to emphasize relationships; the personal is thus prior to the institutional; the institutional exists to nurture and sustain the relations of human persons joined, as far as is possible for us as creatures, in a resemblance to that Trinitarian life. Now it seems to me that if we are to take this starting-point of the Church as a reflection of the Trinitarian life seriously – the *koinonia* of Father, Son and Holy Spirit – then there are some profound and considerable implications for us so far as our under-standing of the being and nature of the Church is concerned – that is ourselves – and thus for the order and structures of the Church. It is interesting to note that this image and metaphor of the Church as *koinonia* has become very much a part of the contemporary currency of ecumenical discourse, where the starting-point with regard to any discussions about Church, whether it be between Churches or within a Church or denomination, is that which is perceived both as gift and promise: the grace of our Lord Jesus Christ, the love of God and the fellowship of the Holy Spirit; the Trinitarian ground and being of the Church and the churches ... the Trinitarian ground of our baptism into the one Lord and Saviour of us all. Through identification with the death and resurrection of Jesus Christ by the power of the Holy Spirit, Christians enter into fellowship with God and with one another in the life and love of God. This fellowship is the mystery of the Church.

There are numerous references to the use of this word *koinonia* in the New Testament, usually translated 'fellow-ship', which in the English language really fails to grasp the profundity and profligacy which is both the gift and generosity of God and which is contained in its original Greek form and crucial to its interpretation. It is about 'participation', not simply Church as a society on earth but also in heaven – participation in the very life of which God is the being and source. I am aware, however, that as I speak of this concept/image of the Church as *koinonia* as being fundamental, nevertheless to concentrate on this particular image of the Church to the exclusion of all others would be a grave mistake.

For in the past I suspect that difficulties have arisen, differences occurred, divisions caused, by seizing upon one model alone to the exclusion of all others.

Indeed, one of the major criticisms of the Report published some five years ago now – *Working as One Body* – a report which contained some very radical proposals for change in the structures of the Church of England, now contained in the National Institutions Measure, and evidenced by the existence of the Archbishops' Council – was based very substantially on the well-known and certainly important Pauline image of the Church as the Body of Christ. However, in so concentrating on this one image, though the Trinitarian image of *koinonia* did receive at least one passing mention, there were those who criticized the whole thrust of the Report in that it rested altogether too much on the image of the Church as the Body of Christ, and the possible dangers of this being interpreted in too stark a 'headship' way. This was perceived to be pushing the Body of Christ image too far – a top-down approach – altogether too hierarchical. 'Carey's curia' was one of the phrases used at one stage (and there remain still considerable concerns about these new arrangements), an approach which was and is alien to an Anglican understanding both of the Church and of its structures and authority. On the other hand, you could argue that Paul's use of *kephale* ought not to be understood in a strictly 'headship' fashion, primarily therefore about rule with its implied authoritarianism, but rather *kephale* as a translation of the Hebrew *reshith*, which is to be understood more fundamentally as beginning, source, the fount out of which things flowed; in other words quite the opposite of 'top down' but rather 'bottom up'.

However, this particular illustration makes my point very well. If we seize upon one image and one image only of the Church, as well as only one interpretation, then we are bound to get it wrong. Other New Testament images are required if we are to ensure proper checks and balances, and as well to appreciate something of the rich 'fullness' of how we are to understand and experience 'Church'. Certainly, since the 'body' model is so predominant in the Pauline understanding and theology, we do need to retain it, just as we do our understanding of the Church as communion. Both of these images rightly and vitally express and enhance the relational nature of the Church – reciprocity and mutuality – the complementarity of gifts and ministries working together as one body in the service of the Church for the sake of the world. We certainly need to hold on to these as we look towards the twenty-first century.

There are, as well, the more overtly dynamic images which I believe we need to recover for our understanding of the Church – a Church which has for too long and too much been wedded to a more static institutional model. Much of the New Testament, and certainly the Acts of the Apostles, envisages Christians as a people on the way and the Church as a pilgrim people. This was certainly one of the key themes to emerge from the Second Vatican Council. At 1 Peter 2.11 we read: 'I beseech you as aliens and exiles'. The words are *paroikos* and *parepidemos*. They are, in fact, words commonly used in Greek and they describe persons who are only temporarily resident in a place and whose home is elsewhere. They are used to describe the patriarchs in their wanderings, and especially Abraham who went out not knowing where he was to go and whose search was for the city whose maker and builder is God (Hebrews 11.9–13). They are used to describe the children of Israel when they were slaves and strangers in the land of Egypt before they entered into the Promised Land (Acts 7.6). I am reminded, too, in this context of that magnificent 'purple' passage, the description of Christian life in the second century in *The Epistle to Diognetus*:

> they live in countries of their own, but simply as sojourners; they share the life of citizens, they endure the lot of foreigners; every foreign land is to them a fatherland, and every fatherland a foreign land ... they spend their existence upon earth, but their citizenship is in heaven.

Here, then, is a clear emphasis on temporariness and transition, on movement and progression and travelling 'light' – a much needed contrast and counterpoint to the Church as a static and fixed institution. Further, to conceive of the Church as a pilgrim people must raise questions for us about the nature of our structures. Of course, for any group or organization, institutional arrangements are inevitable and necessary. The difficulty and the danger arises when these very institutional arrangements become ends in themselves, when they themselves dictate the nature, shape and function of the organization. It is a warning that structures need to be kept to a minimum and that we must constantly be asking questions about what we need at the centre, to which the response can only be 'as little as possible, and only that which manifestly and absolutely cannot be done and effected more locally'. In any case it might be worth asking, 'Where is the centre?'

A further model which I believe is helpful to us and which must surely constantly inform our understanding of the Church is that of herald: a Church charged with the responsibility of proclaiming the Good News, of following the example of its Lord in preaching Good News to the poor (Luke 4. 18ff.). This at once draws our attention both to the content of the proclamation and the ways and means of proclamation. The teaching function of the Church – catechesis, nurture, instruction, learning – is a vital enterprise for the Church today, not least among our young people. There are a variety of ways and means in which we need to engage with the world beyond the Church, and in which we need to learn from one another. Included in this image, the Church as herald, must surely be the prophetic calling of the Church to act as salt and light and leaven – a people who are prepared to challenge poverty, inequality, injustice; to be a voice for the voiceless; a Church itself ready to embrace an altogether more incisive asceticism – that theology of 'enoughness' of which the last Lambeth Conference spoke in the interests of sustainability and survival. The Church as herald, as prophet, is charged with that outward looking engagement with the world; it begins to extend and enlarge our understanding of relationality. It is about evangelization as engagement: engagement not only with each other within the household of faith, but the household of faith with the community and world in which it is set. Clearly, there is implied here the currently much used image of the Church as servant. Just as Christ came into the world to be served and not to serve, so the Church, mirroring the mission of the Saviour, seeks to serve the world by looking and going out beyond itself to celebrate the presence of God already in the world. Bonhoeffer in his *Letters and Papers from Prison* makes the point very clearly when he writes: 'The Church is the Church only when it exists for others ... the Church must share in the secular problems of ordinary human life, not dominating, but helping and serving.' Again, I remember reading Harvey Cox, some long time ago now, and in his *The Secular City* he writes: 'The Church's task ... is to be the *diakonos* of the city, the servant who bends himself to struggle for its wholeness and health.' Or again, John Robinson in his *New Reformation* characterizes something of the more radical nature of such imagery: 'The house of God is not the Church but the world. The Church is the servant, and the first characteristic of a servant is that he lives in someone else's house, not his own.'

Here in this servant theology and ecclesiology is a very necessary corrective to an ecclesiology arising out of a sharply stated view of the Church as the Body of Christ in which 'head' is interpreted in a hierarchical way and where the Church both proclaims and delivers salvation to the world; as opposed to the Church in its ministry and service in the world discovering and celebrating the presence and the activity of God already in it.

I have, then, set out this morning five images/models of the Church: as communion/*koinonia*, Body of Christ, pilgrim people, herald, servant. Here, I suggest, is a constellation of models – not exhaustive – in which no one has an exclusive position or place but where each is held in counterpoise with the other and where all will better inform who and what we are as 'Church' in the twenty-first century. They speak to us as much about the future to which we are all called as the past we have inherited. Furthermore, they temper as well as challenge a heavily institutional and institutionalized view of the Church, and not least those structures which any institution must necessarily have in order as it were to bind it together rather than bind it altogether, and to build it up rather than to weigh it down. Such structures will be light; not overbearing but liberating. The centre, properly understood, must surely be multi-polar – that is at once the myriad manifestations of the One Holy Catholic and Apostolic Church in every place as much as it is diocese, province, world-wide communion. For there could be no meaning whatever to such terms without the communities, the centres, the localities of which they comprise and in which they subsist.

It is Karl Rahner who, writing, almost twenty years ago now, foresaw a future in which the Church would be a 'diaspora-church', no longer necessarily either favoured or supported by 'a homogeneous public opinion, by laws it has itself inspired, by a general acceptance of the position of its leaders'. He speaks of a Church less 'established' (in the institutional sense) and more a 'community' and where much will depend on the assent of faith freely given from below than imposed from above. Here certainly is a much more 'relational' model and where much will depend on the life and style – indeed the lifestyle – of the local as a reflection of the One Holy Catholic and Apostolic Church. Such sentiments find an echo in some more recent writing from a very different source. A female Baptist minister who has worked as Mission Adviser for the Baptist Union of Great Britain concludes in an article entitled *New Ways of Being Church*,

> The future is relational and in general the models seem to be small ... the fact is that the future for the church is much more varied ... enabling the vulnerable and the marginalised to be at the core of church life is a practice which fundamentally affects the way we do church ... leadership models are challenged by less formal gatherings because activity is more shared and participative ... it is interesting that many of the new ways of being church are currently led by women;

and her final sentence – 'We need to watch the margins; the inner cities, the rural areas, where creative approaches are emerging often born in despair.' And indeed I know from my own experience in my own considerable Diocese of York as well the dioceses of the Northern Province that new models and new patterns both of being Church and of mission and ministry are emerging both in the urban and in the rural areas. I well recognize, too, some of the difficulties, frustrations and paradoxes which can arise, but unless we are prepared to take risks and begin to encourage altogether new ways of doing things we shall, I suspect, surely be overtaken by the sheer inertia of doing nothing. I am rather reminded at this point of the response by those two churchwardens in a certain parish when the bishop enquired about their plans for mission – 'Its our inertia that keeps us going here, bishop,' they responded!

Not only are there questions about the structures, organization and governance of our Church, there are, too, questions about institutions – institutions quite other than the Church. In a culture which appears increasingly individualistic and altogether more mobile, paradoxically the search for being and meaning and belonging has become more acute. Often the wish is expressed – 'Oh, if it were only possible to start again' – *tabula rasa* – return to that wistful simplicity and straightforwardness of the early Church ... if only! Fulfilment of such a wish is simply not possible. But what ought to be possible is, in the light and in the context of the reflections I have set out this morning, that the Church should not be forever looking backwards, but rather forward to the future; and, even more importantly, should not be forever fretfully finding more things to do but should rather have the courage more to 'be' – to be still – to stop and look and listen and encourage others so to 'be' – and in so 'being' resonate the more realistically and relevantly with the deep spiritual searchings, yearnings and longings of so many; to enable people the more profoundly and deeply to contemplate the vision of God, the Blessed Trinity, the sheer beauty, the wonder, the splendour, the glory of the God who in Jesus Christ has come among us and in the power of the Holy Spirit dwells in our hearts and in our world.

Here at the heart of it all is a call to holiness – a holiness which is our humanness – each of us made in the image and likeness of God and the Church a place of sanctification and transformation – a people the eyes of whose hearts are enlightened and whose clear confidence is that hope to which God has called us all – 'the riches of His glorious inheritance among the saints'. It brings us back of course to that point from which we set out: the Church as the place where men and women are able to get a taste and catch a glimpse of their eternal eschatological destiny which is communion in God's very life.

So finally a prayer:

148

O God of unchangeable power and eternal light, look favourably on your whole Church, that wonderful and sacred mystery; and by the tranquil operation of your perpetual providence, carry out the work of man's salvation; that things which were cast down may be raised up, and that all things may return to unity through Him by whom all things were made even your Son Jesus Christ our Lord.

Twenty Eight

150th Anniversary of Manchester University

Manchester Cathedral – Wednesday, 21 March 2001

'Get wisdom, and whatever you get, get insight' (Proverbs 4.7)

In his will dated 31 May 1845 John Owens bequeathed the residue of his personal estate to certain trustees for

> the foundation of an institution within the Parliamentary borough of Manchester, or within two miles of any part of the limits thereof, for providing or aiding the means of instruction and improving young persons of the male sex ... in such branches of learning and science as are now and may be hereafter usually taught in the English Universities.

Accordingly, Owens' College was founded and five years later opened in 1851. It was the beginnings of the University of Manchester now comprising some twenty thousand full-time students of whom some four thousand are pursuing postgraduate study and research. In the words of the Vice-Chancellor's message in *Manchester Graduate 2000*, 'The University has come a long way since its humble beginnings ... John Owens would have been proud.'

Two hundred or so years earlier, in 1640, there had, of course, been an abortive attempt to establish a very similar institution here in Manchester. A petition presented to the Long Parliament told of what it described as the 'many ripe and hopeful wits' of the north 'being utterly lost for want of education'. Furthermore – and as a Yorkshireman, born and bred, it pains me somewhat to have to admit it – Manchester, magnificent Manchester, was presented as the 'fittest place for such a foundation ... it being almost the centre of these northern parts ... a town of great antiquity ... a place of fame and ability ... its situation, provision of food, fuel and buildings' all comprising to make it as 'happy a town' as any 'in the northern parts of the kingdom'. Today, three hundred and sixty years after that failed attempt and one hundred and fifty years after Owens' immense generosity which seized the moment and the initiative, we celebrate with thanksgiving the centre of excellence which both nationally and internationally this University of Manchester now is.

So what of the University? What of its purpose? What of the nature of the institution?

Well, The *Shorter Oxford Dictionary* – always a useful arbiter in these matters – directs us to the very roots of the word 'university' itself and the concept of 'the whole'. A university is above all else a community of persons – certainly persons of diverse and varied interests, pursuits and possibilities – a community of persons of widely differing ethnic, social, cultural and religious backgrounds, a community which readily and gladly celebrates its diversity yet speaks to us of a shared and co-operative enterprise with a sense of common endeavour and a shared sense of value, purpose and aspiration. Moreover, it is a community of relationality, where the institution seeks neither to oppress nor dominate but rather to encourage the enticing, exciting and exhilarating project of study, exploration, education. Education in all its aspects, and where the minority as well as the majority will feel equally included within the whole – and always seeking to care for and to honour and to value the human, spiritual and social dimension of each of its members.

Interestingly, and significantly, it was in 1852, just over a year following the foundation of Owens' College, that John Henry Newman (the bicentenary of whose birth we have been recently celebrating) published his *Idea of a University*. It has, I believe, some important messages for us still. Newman made it quite clear that the aim, end and object of any university could be nothing less than total engagement with the pursuit of knowledge in its widest, fullest and deepest sense: 'knowledge which is its own end ... liberal knowledge'. It is not to be simply a research institute or, for that matter, only a provider of professional training but rather a community of people committed to pursuing the totality of truth and doing so through the widest possible range of disciplines, simply because it is the best thing in the world for human beings to do. And for Newman, this commonality of aim and mutually supportive endeavour – to use his own now rather churchy word – he envisaged as a sort of 'inter-communion'. An inter-communion which 'keeps in check the ambitious and the encroaching; [which] succours and maintains those subjects which from time to time are succumbing under the more popular or more fortunately circumstanced; [an inter-communion] which keeps peace between them all'. And in an increasingly competitive and market-driven world these are words which I suspect we may need to hear somewhat more clearly and loudly today!

Further, as Adrian Hastings so rightly comments:

> I cannot see any greater or more humane responsibility for university leadership today than to re-commit itself to the Newman ideal and to a refusal to go down the road of reshaping universities by a policy of brutal amputation, governed by the norms of immediate financial profitability or particularized research potential. Our self-understanding should be higher and more holistic than that.

Again, Newman speaks of the 'practical end', as he describes it, of a university to be for 'training good members of society', 'cultivating the public mind', 'purifying the national taste', 'supplying true principles to popular enthusiasms', 'giving enlargement and sobriety to the ideas of the age'. It lies in women and men being inspired to lives devoted to the great causes of culture, learning and research; to the pursuit of truth, the truth which embraces the pursuit of freedom and peace and the service of one another for the common good. These are the things surely which give a university its authenticity and which enlighten and enliven its spirit.

The writer of the Book of Wisdom speaks of wisdom as 'a reflection of the eternal light, a spotless mirror of the working of God'. And this is a way of speaking which those early luminaries of Owens' College, all of whom were Newman's contemporaries, would instantly have understood: A. J. Scott, the first Principal; Sandeman, the first Professor of Mathematics; Williamson, the first Professor of Natural History; and Frankland, first Professor of Chemistry who, in a way which was characteristic of them all, felt able to describe their own discipline as exemplifying 'the goodness of the great Creator in the transcendingly beautiful, perfect and harmonious laws which He has impressed upon matter'. This is the voice of a wisdom which is close to the core of reality. This is the wisdom which encompasses insight. How we need so desperately this wisdom in a world where presentation is everything and what you see is what you get!

The getting of this wisdom is, though, for the getting of insight. 'Get wisdom ... get insight ... but above all get insight' – understanding, perception, discernment, vision, that altogether more elusive quality of having the ability to see beneath and beyond the surface of things, to be able to get to the heart of the matter, in the face of the complexities, the paradoxes, the questions and contradictions of our age. With one eye very firmly fixed on the difficulties, the challenges, the opportunities which face us in the here and now, in the thick of it (globalization has many guises) but with the other eye equally clearly focused on the distant view, with a clear sense of direction and purpose; this is a vision which is able to transform the present into the future; a vision which encourages and inspires. This is an embracing and encompassing vision which is able on the one hand to allow and to celebrate prodigious diversity of people and pursuits and yet on the other ensure both a coherence and cohesion which binds everything together and gives this university a sense of shared values, a common purpose, a particular and unique flavour. This is the spirit of the place; its very locality here in Manchester serving as much the local as the national and international; and all of us all the time so co-operating for the well-being and flourishing of all in our society, a paradigm of a world redeemed by God in Christ. Remember those words of

St Ireneus: 'the glory of God is a human person fully alive', fully alive in body, mind and spirit. Over these last one hundred and fifty years a very great many have gone out from this University to make their contribution, to make their mark in this and other local communities, in the nation, in the world. And here I cannot but make mention in particular of those great names with which I myself grew up in the days of my own theological study and which remain with me still. They are the giants on the international stage of Christian and biblical theological endeavour: A. S. Peake, H. H. Rowley, C. H. Dodd, T. W. Manson, Tony Dyson, and still with us in retirement and present among us today, Ronald Preston of whom my predecessor wrote that

His thoroughness, persistence and down to earth approach, coupled with a clear grasp of the strengths and limits of theology have enabled him in the field of social ethics to lead the way among British Christians as a highly respected teacher, writer and spokesman in this much disputed and politically sensitive field.

I thank God, too, for one who influenced me personally, again one of the leading patristic scholars of his time, Bishop Richard Hanson.

Of course, each of you, as we celebrate the 150th anniversary of this University, will have your own memories and thanksgivings – memories and thanksgivings of and for the past; and enriched and enlivened by these are the desires and hopes and aspirations, too, for the future.

The last one hundred and fifty years have seen undreamt-of development, growth and change – a development, growth and change which continues apace into the future, a future bright with promise for this world-class university, supported and sustained as it is by significant and fruitful partnerships and sponsors, and making so significant a contribution to the cultural, economic and social life and development of this city.

Our age desperately needs institutions which will hold the ring. Institutions which live and breathe unity, wholeness and coherence; institutions which are prepared to question and challenge the political shibboleths of the day; institutions

154

which will take both the time and the risk always to encourage the longer term view. True to itself and to the selfless generosity of its founder, this University of Manchester can surely, with proper pride, take its place among the best of them. Pray God that it will continue so to do for many years yet to come.

Twenty Nine

Address for a Memorial Service for those who lost their lives at Great Heck on 28 February 2001

York Minster – Saturday, 31 March, 2001

'For I am sure that neither death, nor life ..., nor things present nor things to come ... nor anything else in all creation, will be able to separate us from the love of God in Christ Jesus our Lord' (Romans 8.38, 39)

It was just this last week that I took the 05.59 from York to King's Cross. It was a cold dark morning, and as usual, once the train was under way, some made their way to the buffet for a tea or coffee and a toasted bacon sandwich; some were already deep into their morning newspaper, some renewed the slumbers from which they had no doubt been so rudely awakened to catch the train at this early hour. It was after all a day just like any other day. And that, no doubt, was how it was on that fateful morning of Wednesday, 28 February – a day just like any other day – at least at the beginning and for some twenty-seven or so minutes, yet from that day onwards a day now etched into our memories as a day which can never be like any other day ever again. As we approached the scene of this searing tragedy, the train itself began to slow down as if, three weeks on, to pay tribute to those who had lost their lives and who were injured in so unexpected and so sudden an accident.

We are here in this Minster which has over the long years of its history been witness to adversity, calamity, disaster which has overtaken in one way or another the people of these parts. Today we are united in sadness and sorrow as we stand alongside those whose loved ones were so suddenly and unexpectedly taken from them. We share their sorrow and grief as we commend their loved ones to the God who created them and us in His likeness and image, and in whose eternal and everlasting love we remain, as St Paul reminds us – whether in life or death, whether in this world or the next – 'nothing can separate us from the love of God in Christ Jesus our Lord'. We pray, too, for all those who have been bereaved as well as those injured, and all who will live with the scars of this day, physical, emotional, spiritual, for the remainder of their lives, that the compassion of God and His healing hand will be upon them and His presence with and around them to sustain and support them in the days ahead.

If there is at all any beacon of brightness in the darkness of this terrible event then it must surely be in the readiness and swiftness and response of the emergency services, their unceasing and tireless efforts in the rescue and relief operation. We take them all so much for granted – that they will be there when needed. And indeed they are; giving of themselves in such circumstances and often at considerable risk and danger to themselves in their service of others – physical, emotional, spiritual. Such a rescue as was witnessed at Great Heck on that day and in subsequent days involved large numbers of people with hugely differing skills and expertise. We saw their working together in a co-ordinated way – a sure sign of how things really could and should and ought to be every day. Neither should we forget the people of Great Heck itself – those living just beneath and at the track side – who woke that morning to the noise of the crash, and in the stunned silence that followed looked out incredulously on the sight before them. They, too, without giving any thought to themselves at once began to do what they could in the shadows of that breaking day and later to be available with practical support to those in the first line of the rescue.

And as the presence here of so many people this morning demonstrates, such an event touches us all. Certainly the management and staff of GNER, coming so hard as it did on the heels of the Hatfield disaster, together with Freightliner (whose colleagues and friends and workmates were involved among those who died and were injured) the whole of the rail industry. Indeed it touched the whole nation and beyond, given the huge media presence. Only this last week I was talking to a family who were at the time on the Costa del Sol. They saw the event reported on the television and they told me how it had cast a shadow over them, indeed over the whole hotel in which they were. That cascade of totally unforeseen and unexpected circumstances on that morning demonstrates to us the frailty and fragility of life in this world which is, in fact, with each one of us every day of our lives.

Then there are the questions, and, in particular, that major question which looms large over every tragic happening and event: Why? Why me? Why us? It was the question in my own mind as, just forty-eight hours later at the breaking of the day, I visited for myself that scene of utter desolation – the tangled mass of wreckage. And at once my thoughts were on the tangled body of Christ on the cross, and where in that moment of deep darkness over the whole earth there was the same shrill question from the crucified: My God – why? And here was God in Christ at the very heart of human lostness, bewilderment, anger and pain. God in Christ in death, yet – and here surely is the very ground of our faith and our hope – a God whom death could not contain and in whose death death itself has been overcome for good and all.

And this is precisely the point which Paul in the passage from his letter to the Romans is determined to make. He does not avoid or evade the harsh realities of life, human life which, as part of its very fabric, has about it a certain precariousness, unknowing, risk – such is the very risk of God in creation itself. In another place Paul speaks of what he describes as 'the groaning and travailing of the whole creation'. Certainly over recent months – first the floods, then rail accidents, now the foot-and-mouth crisis and the nosedive of the money markets – all these things conspire to oppress us and face us with those altogether more profound and ultimate questions about ourselves, our society, our lives and our world. They certainly make us stop and think. And maybe that is exactly what we should be about in a world so starved of those deeper spiritual values – ourselves making time to stop and think and reflect, but not just only now, but as a regular feature of our lives. Again, for Paul this 'groaning and travailing of the whole creation' – embracing all those things which beset and burden and bewilder us from time to time, sometimes to a larger and greater extent – are to be set within the altogether wider landscape of the eternal, and in the sure and certain knowledge of the God who is the beginning and the end of all things; the one who has the whole world in His hands, who has you and me in His hands, eternally, everlastingly. As regularly we recite in our statement of faith – 'we look for the resurrection of the dead and the life of the world to come'. Here is a God who is the God of life, who, as Isaiah reminds us, has swallowed up death for ever. Here is a God the wideness and the wonder of whose love ever surrounds us, is ever held out to us and for us and in whom is our comfort and our consolation.

Yes there was the tangled wreckage early that Friday morning which I still remember so vividly. But there was also on the horizon the first signs of the dawn of a new day, the sky shot with the beams of the morning sun. There in that moment there was the destruction and the desolation of one day, yet giving way to the new hope, the new possibilities, the new life of another. In God's perspective, His endless and eternal day – a day where there is no more sadness and sorrow, a day which, in the brightness and the joy of His presence for ever and always, an altogether new creation, lost in wonder, love and in praise, we shall see God as He is and in His presence find our truest and our fullest fulfilment.

To the same God, from whose love in Christ nothing can separate us, be all honour and glory, now and to the end of the ages. Amen.

Thirty

Easter Day

York Minster – 15 April 2001

'The angel said ... He is not here; he has risen ... go quickly and tell his disciples ... he has risen ... he is going before you' (Matthew 28. 5–7)

So Matthew tells of the greatest and most significant event in human history – the resurrection of Jesus Christ from the dead. And Easter Day is the occasion when, year on year, Christian people throughout the world – and on this day, significantly, Christians of every tradition both East and West on the same day – celebrate this Good News for then, for now, for all time and for all people. The news itself, as on that first Easter morning, is greeted with sharply differing reactions. Matthew speaks both of the fear and of the joy of the disciples. Mark concludes his Gospel with terror and amazement. Luke tells us of their astonishment; John of the shocked surprise of Mary Magdalene. And the differing reactions reflect and anticipate to some extent the responses of every person in every age to the event of Jesus' resurrection: both awesome mystery as well as historical fact. The women at the tomb are told to go and 'tell his disciples'. The disciples themselves are told – 'Go out into all the world'. For here is a message and a mission which is from God, God's word to the world in every age. The disciples and successive generations of Christians after them have responded to Christ's own command to go with considerable alacrity and at times with great courage and heroism, all too often at the cost of their own lives.

The martyrs of the early days – as with the martyrs of the twentieth century, women and men – have given themselves and their lifeblood in testimony to the Good News which today we celebrate. Furthermore, here was no merely 'spiritual' message which they sought to deliver to the world and its people. Rather it was a message about God's continuing work in His world: to heal, to reconcile, to restore. Furthermore, it was not only a message confined to and for the Church. It was rather a challenge to the Church that it should be out and about in God's world declaring His truth, His justice, His righteousness and, in itself and its life, the Church, Christian people, Christian communities and congregations already living the values and the qualities of the kingdom. It is this same Easter faith which has been for so many a beacon of light and hope in times of darkness and despair; in times of oppression, strife and war; in times of pain and anguish, of suffering and grief. Some of the most powerful expressions of Christ's resurrection have emerged from those so oppressed and overwhelmed.

Over recent months in the country as a whole and certainly here in the north and North Yorkshire, people have certainly felt oppressed and downcast – first the floods and their aftermath with numbers of people still unable to return to their homes – then the rail crashes, both affecting people travelling on the East Coast mainline, and the Great Heck disaster very close indeed to home. Then the current foot-and-mouth crisis, the world-wide economic uncertainty in which, inescapably, our own economy is caught up – all this, together with the stresses and strains of daily life, have caused people generally to start questioning (and not least our young people): What is going on? Where are we going? And, indeed, to raise some of the more profound questions about life, its meaning, its purpose.

And perhaps we should do well to stay with some of these questions which are in a sense as old as the human race itself, yet questions which are inescapable in every age for they are a part of the fragility, frailty and finiteness and our humanness, in the context of God's order and creation.

The resurrection of Jesus Christ, far from shirking such questions, rather faces them head on and sets them in a wider and larger context. It transforms them and us into the perspective of the overarching purposes of God from beginning to end: His purposes of creation, redemption, salvation. Here in Christ who is risen is the touchstone of light in darkness, of hope in despair, of triumph in tragedy. Here is the truth that the God who in Jesus Christ has entered into our deepest darkness is the one who also gives us hope for ourselves and our world, who leads us into the light, into the bright beams of His endless day.

The event of Christ's resurrection which today we celebrate with great joy encompasses past, present and future. Yes, it is an event in the past. At the heart of each of the Gospel accounts there is the surprised discovery by the women on that first Easter Day that the unexpected and totally unprecedented had happened – Jesus Christ whom they had buried in the tomb on the evening of Good Friday now stood before them in the garden. The tomb was empty: Christ was risen. But it is an event also for the present. Christ is risen, this day and every day. For there in that once-upon-a-time event is a once-and-for-all-time event. The resurrection of Jesus Christ can never be reversed, undone, eradicated. The freedom for life, the transforming power of the same Good News continues in the Church, through the Church, by the Church for the sake of the world. What other motive or reason could there be for those who are still prepared in self-sacrificial ways to give of themselves and their lives wholly in the service of others? Those working even now in situations of loneliness and isolation; those who are devoting themselves to working with homeless people; among the drug addicts and the alcoholics; those who deliberately choose in the name of Christ to place themselves at the margins and beyond so that they might bring something of that abundance of life which Christ wills for all to all. Those who are still prepared to risk themselves and their families in missionary endeavour to work in places of considerable danger; those who are called into the particular life of a religious community to live out vows of poverty, chastity and obedience.

So, too, are each of us called on this Easter Day to be what through our baptism and our participation in this Holy Communion we are as St Peter in his First Epistle describes it – 'A chosen race, a royal priesthood, a holy nation, God's own people in order that you may proclaim the mighty acts of

Him who called you out of darkness into His marvellous light'. It is a summons to the making known of Jesus Christ out there in God's world day by day on the part of each and every one of us truly to live His risen life. The resurrection of Jesus is both a past event and a present reality. Today, we are risen with Christ. It is also hope for the future. In fact the truth is that the resurrection *is* the future of God's glory and God's eternity already with us in this present.

Given the demands and preoccupations with the immediacy of the present that most of us experience, and given that we become so utterly immersed in the increasing drivenness of the now, the resurrection of Jesus Christ bids us raise our hearts and our eyes to that altogether larger and fuller vision and to see this present and all that it encompasses: the happinesses and the joys as well as the pains, the struggles, the frustrations and the difficulties, in the light of eternity. As that wonderful prayer has it 'That we may so pass through things temporal that we finally lose not the things eternal'.

So, far from being so focused on our lives in this world, we are called to see ourselves and our world in the light of God's loving and eternal purposes for us and for his entire creation. 'Strive first for the kingdom of God and His righteousness, and all these things will be added unto you' warns this same Gospel of Matthew. We need to be attentive to those deeper spiritual values which strengthen and sustain us not just as Christians but as the human persons we are and in the neighbourhoods and communities we live – our own aliveness, but the abundant aliveness of others too.

Today, as with every Sunday, is the first day of the week. It is the first day of the rest of our lives. This ancient and venerable Minster has witnessed many Easters in very differing circumstances and situations, but perhaps none more so significant than on Easter Eve in the year 627 when Paulinus baptized Edwin King of Northumbria, and Christianity itself was reborn and flourished in these northern parts. The challenge, the task of the Church today, remains the same. Like those first disciples, as with Paulinus and the successive generations who have come here on this day – ourselves – to live out the wonderful works of Him who has called us out of darkness into His marvellous light: *the* truth about Jesus

Christ, the same yesterday, today and for ever; and in so doing, to enable many others to make the surprised, astonished and joyful discovery that Christ is risen. He was dead but now He is alive for evermore.

Thirty One

Institute of Management (Cumbria Branch) 25th Public Annual Celebrity Lecture – The Business of Ethics

You may recall the apocryphal story about the unpredictable and thoroughly inept young subaltern whose military career was rapidly developing into a series of disasters of dazzling and epic proportions. In weary resignation his Commanding Officer was driven to write on the young man's annual confidential report 'This officer's men will follow him anywhere – if only out of sheer curiosity!'

The prospect of an archbishop launching himself into the deep waters of business and finance, the market economy and globalization must hold for you who know just how deep, complex and sometimes treacherous these waters can be, something of the same slightly morbid fascination. Will he sink – or will he swim?! Is there going to be a meeting of minds between us, or is confusion going to be the worse confounded?

As it was, for example, when a certain gentleman telephoned his bank. 'I would like,' he asked, 'to make some changes to my holdings.' The person on the other end of the telephone requested further details. 'Certainly, sir, but are you interested in conversion or redemption?' 'Good heavens,' came the brisk response, 'I must have got the wrong number! I wanted the Bank of England not the Church of England!'

But, back to my title – The Business of Ethics. Various suggestions have been made, resulting in The Business of Ethics, though with the expanded explanation beneath – that what we are about this evening is a time 'to pause and to think about the moral principles which should guide any business'. Before I go any further I should just like to pause for a few moments on those two key words – 'business' and 'ethics'.

The Oxford English Dictionary – the shorter version – comprises quite a lengthy entry under the word 'business'. It speaks of 'the state of being busily engaged in anything' – activity, briskness – care, attention, diligent labour'. The word begins to be used in the fifteenth century of a stated occupation, profession or trade. By the eighteenth century it has become regular in usage for trade, commercial transactions or engagements, and that basically remains the broad meaning of the word as it continues to be used today: trade, industry, commerce and so on. 'Ethics' derives from a Greek word which fundamentally speaks of character and manner, in the sense of 'manners maketh man'. Ethics, of course, has a long and distinguished history in ancient Greece itself. The names of Socrates, Aristotle and Plato in particular come to mind, as they reflect and philosophize on the meaning of such words as 'good', 'just', 'temperate'. Remember Plato's four cardinal virtues: justice, courage, moderation of desire and practical insight. The word 'ethics' speaks also of disposition and temper – that is, attitude and disposition. It is, in other words, a word which itself is ethical/moral. 'Ethos' is one of its correlates. You might just ask yourselves what is the ethos of your company, your organization? Is there a word or a phrase which more immediately springs to mind which describes the reality of who you are and what you are about in your business? The dictionary definition goes on to speak of 'the rules of conduct recognized in certain departments of human life'. And in the late seventeenth century it comes to be used of 'the science of human duty in its widest extent, the science of law whether civil, political or international'. So much then for dictionary definitions, but already you will gather that they begin to give us some helpful clues about these two major words which comprise the title of my lecture this evening. 'The Business of Ethics and the Ethics of Business' was the longer title which preceded this shortened version. And whilst it certainly seemed to be altogether too cumbersome for any poster or advertisement, this longer title does identify rather more effectively the essential character of what I wish to set before you, as well as establishing the very necessary and, in my view, crucial relationship which there is between those two words: 'business' and 'ethics'.

The title of my presentation this evening takes up this challenge and poses a very major question: Does ethics have anything at all to do with business and if so why and what?

There are those who would argue that, like oil and water, business and ethics simply do not mix. As F. R. Barry, a former Bishop of Southwell, in his book *Christian Ethics and Secular Society*, writes: 'the cynical phrase "business is business" is a trespassing notice: morality keep out'. But rightly, in my view, he then goes on to argue that ethics simply cannot accept that conclusion. 'Business,' he writes, 'after all, is a human activity, and must therefore always have moral relevance and, like every other human activity, is answerable to the sovereignty of God.' So a Christian bishop and moral theologian writing in 1966. It would have come as a considerable surprise therefore to him, I suspect, to have received a copy of *The Economist* of 22–28 April 2000 and to have discovered there a substantial article with the title 'Business Ethics – Doing Well by Doing Good – Does Virtue Pay?' Put another way, I noted a headline in the Money section of *The Sunday Times* of 16 July last year – 'Is vice more preferable than virtue?' – an article about pension funds and what were described as 'unethical' firms. It would be interesting to pose the question to you all: Which businesses do you consider to be 'ethical' or 'unethical', and what might your criteria be for so concluding? The article in *The Economist* began with the same dilemma as already I have myself elaborated: to many people the very concepts of 'business' and 'ethics' sit uneasily together. Business ethics, to them, is an oxymoron, or, as an American journalist once put it, a contradiction in terms like 'jumbo' or 'tiger' shrimp. And yet in America and other western countries companies increasingly wonder what constitutes ethical corporate behaviour and how to get their employees to observe it. Management schools teach courses on the subject to their students.

'Business ethics is suddenly all the rage', so *The Economist*. Indeed the general thrust of the article was that ethics is now perceived to be a number one priority, where Corporate Ethics Officers have become *de rigueur*, at least for the big corporations. United Technologies, for example, boast an international network of no less than 160 Business Ethics Officers. And in what areas do these good people advise? Well, as you would expect, on matters of sexual equality, race relations, workers rights; but also on that tricky sort of management problem as, for example, when an individual who is a wonderful producer, a dedicated worker, who more importantly contributes very significantly to the company profits yet who does not adhere to the company's values. In other words, when a company has to decide whether to sack an employee who is productive but naughty. Again, what do you do, for example, as a line manager when already you know that one of your team is about to take out an enormous mortgage but you are also informed that the person is about to be made redundant, but apparently you are not allowed to tell the person so? Or what do you do when your boss lies to you? The article in *The Economist* notes 'that's a big one!'

But, then, there are many more, apparently regarded 'mundane matters'. A few pens go missing from the office; one of your employees uses the telephone for private calls; the Internet has a particular attraction for a number in work time, and so on. Does it matter? Does it matter if a few pens go missing? (Half those surveyed in a major article in *Management Today*, January 2001 – 'Ethics at work, where do you drawn the line?' – thought not.) Does it matter if profit figures are massaged, so long as no money is stolen? (And it seems that one in ten board directors thought that it did not.) Does any of it matter? Does it matter who gets ripped off so long as we can get away with it? Are profits everything, no matter how they are achieved?

The *Management Today* ethics survey – some of you may have read it – posed the question: what would you do in the following theoretical situation? Jim takes a taxi to a business meeting. He has plenty of time and he could have gone by public transport, which is quite reliable where he lives, for £1.40. At the end of the cab journey which costs £4.50 to which

Jim adds a 50p tip, the cab driver offers him a receipt for £4.50, excluding tip, or a receipt for £5.00 which covers the fare and the tip, or a blank receipt. Jim accepts the blank receipt, fills it in for £6.50 and claims it on expenses. Apparently just over 50 per cent saw the tip as a legitimate expense and that seems to me to be fair enough. A more prudent 35 per cent thought that Jim should have used public transport instead, and I myself would have inclined to that view. Only a tiny minority were prepared to exploit the situation and make a fraudulent claim. Yet on the same page it is reported that 40 per cent of people believe that there is no real difference between fraud and a bit of expense fiddling. seventy-five per cent thought it was acceptable to make personal phone calls from work; 48 per cent believed it was acceptable to take pens and pencils from work; 22 per cent thought it was acceptable to surf the Net for pleasure in work time; 17 per cent thought it was acceptable to use company petrol for personal mileage and 15 per cent thought it was acceptable to take software home. The article concluded that these were 'shocking figures'. Perhaps an altogether more revealing finding of the survey was that fewer than 50 per cent felt that people at the top are strong ethical role models. Now, inevitably of course, the scope of such a survey will necessarily be somewhat limited and circum-scribed, it does, nevertheless, I believe, highlight some serious concerns which are inescapably 'ethical'. It was interesting to note that whilst those interviewed believe this whole area of ethics to be somewhat complex, nevertheless eight out of ten indicated that they thought it was sufficiently important to be given some training on the subject. The article concluded: 'If this survey achieves anything it will at least encourage those who have the power and authority to effect change in the workplace culture to answer the call.' Perhaps a similar conclusion may be drawn at the end of this lecture.

You may just also be wondering what all this has to do with the Church. Management and business are one thing, the Church should confine itself to the things which are more properly its domain, namely the spiritual, and let the managers get on with what is properly theirs, namely the things of this world which the Church can never or will never fully understand or comprehend. After all, as the good book has it, 'You cannot serve God and mammon'. In the same way, I hear many responding to the Church's comments in the political arena. Yet this is precisely the point at which there needs to be engagement rather than estrangement. For at the heart of the Christian faith is the belief in a God who became incarnate – a God who has come among us in Jesus Christ. That is the whole point of the celebration of the third millennium – the incarnation of God – the material and the spiritual; the eternal and the temporal – welded together for ever and always. So it is never possible for the Churches or the Christian faith to make any separation between the two. If we are truly to fulfil the creator's purposes for us then there has to be a knitting together and a working together both of the spiritual and the material – the one in dialogue, in understanding, in conversation and in critique with the other. And this perhaps leads us into one of the first basic principles which I should like to set before you this evening. For if Bishop Barry's statement, which I quoted right at the very beginning of this lecture, is right, as it surely must be, namely that business is as much to do with people as it is to do with things, commodities, trade, IT and so on – then one very basic starting-point must be a recognition of the status of each and every human person.

I think I can do no better than set before you in this regard a brief extract from *The Common Good*: a statement on the social teaching of the Roman Catholic Church published just before the last General Election. It is certainly a statement which I would think could be endorsed by every Christian denomination and group.

> We believe each person possesses a basic dignity that comes from God, not from any human quality or accomplishment, not from race or gender, age or economic status. The test therefore of every institution or policy is whether it enhances or threatens human dignity and indeed human life itself. Policies which treat people as only economic units or policies which reduce people to a passive state of dependency on welfare, do not do justice to the dignity of the human person.

So a very appropriate 'ethical' question is posed at once: Does your business/organization do justice to the dignity of the human person – persons individually and persons collectively – involved in your organization? Do you treat people only as economic units or, rather, do you have a fundamental concern not simply for their well-being but for their actual flourishing as persons? It is St Irenaeus who speaks of the human person in the following terms: 'The glory of God is a human person fully alive.'

In York, for example, I am mindful of the initiatives taken by the Rowntree family born of their religious principles, namely, their care for and concern about the whole person – both outside and within the workplace. The same Quaker principles were at work as well with Cadbury in Birmingham: those principles being that the company should improve its workers' health and education, their life and well-being. Perhaps in today's more cynical and competitive world corporate virtue no longer seems a goal in its own right. Again, how do we conceive of our employees, those who work for us and among us, some of them over a long number of years in long-established firms? Again, *The Common Good*:

> Employers need reminding that their employees as a body constitute a form of 'social capital', a reservoir of human effort, wisdom and experience. Accountancy methods which have to disregard such assets in the valuation of a commercial concern or in drawing up a balance sheet are inevitably guilty of false accounting, for they fail to make visible the resources of human skill and judgement that the company has at its disposal. This dumping of human 'social capital' is a prevalent cause of social injustice in modern society. It often occurs in company downsizing operations associated with takeovers, closures and mergers.

I can certainly testify from close friends of mine who have experienced precisely such 'dumping', having given the best years of their lives to a particular enterprise, suddenly to be informed that they are no longer wanted or needed. The way we conceive of people and the way we treat people is also, I would suggest, reflected in the way we reward them. You will recall that one of those very earliest ethical principles of the ancient Greeks was 'justice'. It is a fundamental ethical concept and recurs many times in the Old Testament as a facet and dimension of God's righteousness. It features prominently in the utterances of the prophets and is not very far from 'righteousness' and 'judgement'. In other words, the deeds and words and actions of human persons are to reflect those moral qualities of God's righteousness and God's justice – otherwise God's judgement will ensue.

In this context I take it that we are speaking of what is sometimes termed distributive justice – the kind of justice which attempts to ensure the fair distribution of rights and privileges and rewards on the maxim 'everyone to their due'. The Old Testament account of Moses receiving the law from God saw (in common with other ancient religions) the basis of justice in the will or *fiat* of God. The Stoics in their philosophizing conceived of justice as rooted in the natural (rational) order of things. This is very similar to the doctrine of natural law which sees justice – the justice of God – reflected in the human person of any and every age and the moral quality of the human person whether religious or not. So I would suggest this distributive justice to be an ethical dimension for any business enterprise. It is perhaps more sharply focused in the area of hours and wages. I realize that the minimum wage is a matter of some difference of view. What I am speaking of here is of a just wage. *The Common Good* again:

> Employers ... have a duty to pay a just wage, the level of which should take account of the needs of the individual and not just his or her value on the so-called labour market ... it is not morally acceptable to seek to reduce unemployment by letting wages fall below the level at which employees can sustain a decent standard of living ... employers who pay only the level of wage that the labour market demands, however low, are avoiding their moral responsibilities for the welfare of their employees ... it is to be preferred that employers should understand their duties to their employees correctly so that they should want to pay a just wage regardless of whether they are obliged by the law to do so.

Now clearly there are conflicts here. My own origins are in the West Riding of Yorkshire where both coal and wool were the basic source of industry and of a thriving commercial base. Indeed I can still remember going with my father, who was a builder, and who used to do building works in those days for Paton and Baldwin's – at both their mills in Wakefield – going with him to those mills and the sheer noise of the machines, the greasy floorboards from the wool and the distinctive smell of the place. Part at least of the undermining of the woollen trade was to be attributed to the fact that manufacturing the final product could be achieved far more cheaply in what some would describe as the sweatshops of the southern hemisphere than they could in the more expensive labour markets of our own country. On the international scene, where companies are dealing with several countries such questions as a living wage, a just wage can become certainly complex and difficult. That does not, however, in my view absolve any company from a careful assessment and discussion, which includes the sort of moral and ethical considerations I am currently addressing, from being part of any such decision-making – and, more particularly, the possible knock-on effect here at home and among employees for any decisions so taken.

I have made a passing mention of 'hours'. I am aware of European directives on hours now incorporated into employment law in this country. I sometimes wish such directives applied to me! I suspect many of you will probably be thinking likewise. And quite frankly I just wonder sometimes whether rules and regulations, albeit probably good in themselves, and in some modest measure, do not in the end tend to become rather self-justifying, even self-multiplying! However, I do just wish to point up another moral difficulty in the wake of, for example, Sunday trading. I have to say that I argued at the time very strongly in the House of Lords that we should not proceed with the legislation now in force. I did not wish necessarily to maintain the somewhat arcane arrangements of the fifteenth and sixteenth centuries or indeed of past ages. Neither did I for that matter desire the situation as it currently obtains. But my concern again is with the attitudes of management, some management, to those people who either do not wish to or who simply cannot work on Sundays, either for religious or family or quite other reasons. And the suggestion that shops should now be open on Christmas Day actually beggars belief in my view. Have we really finally succumbed to that which was half coined in jest – Tesco, *ergo sum*! Workers have been pressurized, intimidated, threatened with unemployment and so on if they are not prepared readily to conform to their employers' wishes about Sunday or other extraordinary working hours. Justice again demands that these concerns be heard and properly addressed. The reason why I felt so particularly about Sunday trading was because I was at the time working as a vicar in the West End of London, in a parish which took in part of the northern section of Oxford Street. Saturday evenings came and Sunday mornings dawned – peaceful, quiet. You could almost feel the relief in the buildings and the streets themselves as they breathed a sigh of relief against the almost unrelieved tramplings of people and traffic and noise and pressure.

It was just about a year ago now that I was in the process of leading a pilgrimage of some three hundred or so people to the Holy Land. *Shabat* in Israel remains an institution – thankfully. The fact remains of a slackening of pace beginning on the Friday afternoon as people seek to make their way home for the onset of *Shabat*, home to their families and among their own. Saturday morning dawns, different – peaceful, silent – as if to recall us all to who and what we are as human persons and human beings, made in God's image. The airline ceases to fly. The airport is closed. Inconvenient, maybe, but inconvenient to make an even more important point about our survival as human persons.

There is a link here, I would suggest, with human rights – described in one article as a 'newer and trickier problem'. However, the basic principle of rights for human persons has long been respected in the Christian moral tradition, recognizing that individuals have a claim on each other and on society for certain basic minimum conditions without which the value of human life is diminished or even negated. Such 'rights' are in my view inalienable. The very fundamental right to life, religious liberty, decent work, housing, health care, education, freedom of speech and the right to raise and provide for a family, and, I would add here, in here a right to proper provision for rest, recreation and renewal. However, in the increasing use of the term human rights, which would appear to seek to justify me and my wants, my desires, my fulfilment without any regard whatsoever to anyone or anything else, let alone anyone else's rights, begins to devalue the very concept. Thus the application of rights and the exclusive pursuit of the rights of the individual against an equivalent stress on duty and the requirement to love and serve one's neighbour as oneself soon begins to undermine the very concept of human rights itself. I am aware, however, that the human rights legislation now incorporated into the English legal system is considerably complex and that it is difficult to draw broad and general conclusions without perhaps the greater assemblage of individual cases. In this connection, as well, I recognize just how increasingly litigious our society as a whole is becoming, and where individuals seem a good deal more sensitized to their rights – at least that is the sort of language which I hear being used – than they were.

It was John Wesley in his sermon on 'The Use of Money' in 1744 who urged Christians to 'gain all you can, save all you can, give all you can'. And in this he struck a note which resonates very well with the basic thrust of biblical teaching. For the Bible consistently recognizes the value and importance of a market economy. BUT – and it is a very big 'but' – it was not a market economy left to itself, wholly unfettered and with no constraints whatsoever. The biblical view is very clear: it was a market economy which operated, and which understood itself to be sustained, within a supporting, shaping web of constraints, of moral imperatives. The basic one of course being the golden rule: Thou shalt love the Lord thy God with all thy soul, with all thy heart and with all thy mind and thy neighbour as thyself.

You will recall that it is Adam Smith who in his *The Wealth of Nations* in 1776 is generally reckoned to be the founding father of capitalist theories. The basic thesis of the book is the belief that in an entirely free economy each citizen through seeking his or her own gain would be 'led by an invisible hand to promote an end which was not part of his intention', namely, the prosperity of society. Well, experience does tell us that sometimes this does happen, but to say that it invariably must happen as if by a God-given natural law is a view which can amount to idolatry or a form of economic superstition. Indeed, Smith, himself, did not appear to think that the rule was invariable, for he also observed that the individual, 'by pursuing his own interest he *frequently* promotes that of society'. So whilst the Christian tradition can certainly be shown to be supportive of a market economy, that same tradition equally insists that the end results of market forces must be scrutinized and, if necessary, adjusted in the name of natural law, social justice, human rights and the good of all. *The Common Good* itself insists

> Left to themselves market forces are just as likely to lead to evil results as to good ones. It is often overlooked that Adam Smith himself did not envisage markets operating in a value free society, but assume that individual consumer choices would be governed by moral considerations, not least the demands of justice.

There are wider implications here, too, as *The Common Good* points up:

> Those who advocate unlimited free market capitalism and at the same time lament the decline in public and private morality, to which the encouragement of selfishness is a prime contributing factor, must ask themselves whether the messages they are sending are in fact mutually contradictory. People tend to need more encouragement to be unselfish than to be selfish, so it is not difficult to imagine which of these two messages will have most influence. A wealthy society, if it is a greedy society, is not a good society.

The market economy in its global tumescence has already seen off the command economies and fancies itself well on the way to seeing off the nation state. It is easily conceived as standing colossus-like over the world, and that it has become a self-authenticating process, entire and complete in itself. So pervasively powerful is this image that it is fast becoming a paradigm for human life itself. For when everything that matters can be bought and sold; when shopping becomes worship and advertising slogans its litany; when our worth as human beings is measured by what we earn and what we spend – when this happens, are not all values reducible to profit and loss? And is not the bottom line devoid of space for things like love, patience, self-sacrifice, trust and hope? Are we not in danger of squeezing out those very things which belong to our peace? Furthermore, as the Chief Rabbi so well observes, 'It encourages a view of human life itself as a series of consumer choices rather than as a set of inherited ways of doing things.'

More than that, are we not so ascribing to 'money', however that is to be interpreted, a God-like quality, that very idolatry so vehemently denounced in both Old and New Testaments – and in so doing to reduce the precious gift that God makes to us of each other, each one of us made in His image and likeness, to mere things: at worst pawns rather than persons? Yet in saying this I must emphasize yet again that the Judaeo/Christian tradition is not against the market economy *per se* and as a matter of principle. Indeed I have attempted to demonstrate that, given certain ethical and moral parameters in structuring creation as he has, God has given tacit approval and encouragement to the entrepreneurial process. It is a process which brings with it rich potential for the advancement of human well-being – and anyone who has doubts about that might care to reflect on, say, his prospects for continued health without the benefits of modern sanitation or without the products of the pharmaceutical companies. These are great benefits, but they are benefits which stand in great danger of being compromised by that hubris which would define humanity solely in terms of the market place. Bread we must have, but we shall not live by bread alone. The notion that we should do so is, again in the words of the Chief Rabbi, 'one of the great corrosive acids which eats away at the girders upon which society rests'.

I cannot help reflecting that when that report *Faith in the City* first appeared well over ten years ago now, rubbished at the time (of course leaked ahead of its publication date) by one government minister as Marxist, there were two key phrases: 'encouraging enterprise' and 'promoting partnership', ironically the very phrases which very latterly became the mantras of the Conservative government and which figure prominently in present government pronouncements. Religion points towards the eternal verities which lie beyond space and time; the market place declares that we are set in the here and now. We cannot and we must not allow either of these to become so polarized that they simply do not engage the one with the other.

Germane, I believe, to the subject matter of my lecture this evening are those seven principles of public life set out by the Nolan Commission. Maybe they give us something of a framework for a code of ethics in business – the very business of ethics. The development of a more formal ethical policy can, however, be somewhat tricky. It can raise some awkward questions. As, for example, when the chairman of a large British firm recalled how his company secretary, a lawyer, decided to draft an ethics code with appropriately lofty standards. 'You do realize', said the chairman, 'that if we publish this, we will be expected to follow it. Otherwise our staff and customers may ask questions.' Somewhat downcast, the lawyer secretary went off to produce something really rather more attuned to reality. Such codes in my experience are more often than not too broadly general and aspirational to be of any real practical guidance and use. Of course, perhaps the best example of such a type of code is the Ten Commandments – itself paralleled in the ancient world with numerous other similar 'moral' codes – as, for example, the Law Code of Hammurabi – pretty primitive, no doubt, but nevertheless intended both for the good of the individual and as well for the community and the whole of society. *The Economist* article has the following comment:

> The best corporate codes, says Robert Solomon of the University of Texas, are those that describe the way everybody in the company already behaves and feels. The worst are those where senior executives mandate a list of principles – especially if they then fail to 'walk the talk' themselves. However, he says, 'companies debate their values for many months, but they always turn out to have similar lists'. There is usually something about integrity; something about respect for the individual; and something about honouring the customer.

178

You will recall that the seven principles set out by Lord Nolan's Commission are as follows: selflessness, integrity, objectivity, accountability, openness, honesty, leadership. Now if in terms of leadership and management these principles are to be applied to yourselves what are the implications? Very considerable, I would suggest. And whether you like it or not, a very great deal does flow from the manner and the style of the person at the top. That is why, for example, it is so vital that we have persons of the highest calibre as head teachers in our schools. They set the tone, the ethos, the culture – you can tell almost as soon as you enter a school. Similarly, the parson in the parish and so on. So what then of these seven principles – how might they shape some sort of code which, whilst general in nature, could then in particular situations and circumstances, organizations, businesses be more finely honed and tuned into what John Adair might describe as clear and realistic targets. Selflessness speaks of decisions to be taken not in order to gain financial or other material benefits for oneself but again in the common good. Integrity speaks of a certain rectitude, uprightness, a coherence and cohesion, a soundness, lack of corruption. Again, a dictionary definition: 'soundness of moral principles; the character of uncorrupted virtue; uprightness, honesty, sincerity'. Lord Nolan's statement is that holders of public office should not place themselves under any financial or other obligation to outside individuals or organizations that might influence them in the performance of their official duties. There are parallels equally here, I would suggest, whether public or private.

Objectivity is about carrying out business, including making appointments, awarding contracts or recommending individuals for rewards and benefits. All such decisions are to be made on merit – not on the old boy or any other network for that matter. The word objectivity surely speaks for itself. As for accountability, as we expect our employees to be accountable to us there must surely be a complementarity of accountability, namely that we ourselves are also accountable for our decisions and actions and ought to be ready to submit ourselves to whatever scrutiny is appropriate to our particular office. Are we sufficiently accountable? Again in terms of openness and transparency it is important that we should be as open as possible about all decisions and actions that we take. Good reasons should be given for decisions and the restriction of information should be confined to those situations and circumstances only when such restriction is absolutely necessary.

It hardly needs me surely to have to underline the word honesty. Honesty in thought, in word and in deed. There was a time when you could say a gentleman's word is his guarantee. In other words, what he said he held to and honoured. Again, I can remember my father and the way he operated. Old fashioned and long ago that may now be, but if a price was agreed over the telephone or face to face in a conversation that was that. Indeed, people so trusted him, I remember, that they simply never bothered to request a confirmation in writing. They knew that he would honour his words – and sometimes I have to say at considerable loss to himself. Sadly and increasingly that seems to be no longer possible.

And finally, of course, leadership. It brings us back to 'walking the talking', to use the American slang phrase. Leadership by example. Moreover, leadership does not exist as in a vacuum. The leader, the chairman, the manager, the chief executive, the line manager, whoever you may be and at whatever level in the organization, you as an individual exist in relationship – in relationship to others both vertically and horizontally. As John Adair, in his book with the challenging title *Not Bosses But Leaders*, so clearly enunciates, 'Effective leadership has an end product – the high performance team.' And remember they say that a conductor is only as good as the orchestra. John Adair sets out seven marks for a high performance team. I myself have found them extremely helpful in the ordering of my own teams – as Bishop in Wakefield, London and now York. They are as follows, and I commend them to you for your further reflection. He describes them as 'hallmarks':

- clear realistic objectives;
- shared sense of purpose;
- best use of resources;
- atmosphere of openness;
- reviews progress;
- builds on experience;
- rides out storms.

180

I must begin to draw my lecture to some conclusion. It has, I admit, ranged somewhat far and wide, but at least it has, I believe, touched on some important and salient areas in the whole area of business and ethics. However, before I conclude I wish to state that I must confess my own failings and shortcomings before you in this context and where I am unable to present myself before you as totally unblemished in this regard. The context of my first shortcoming, if it may so be described, is eastern Europe – Romania to be precise – in the early part of the Ceaucescu regime in 1967. I had been appointed Anglican Chaplain in Romania, Bulgaria and Yugoslavia but was to live in Romania. I needed an 'unlimited' entry and exit visa in order to travel from Romania from time to time into Yugoslavia and Bulgaria. The person at the Romanian Patriarchate when first I approached him said 'impossible', but at the same time started to shrug his shoulders, rubbing his thumb and forefinger together and saying perhaps well it might just be possible but come back in two days. In two days I went back, presented my passport and papers with the same request though having secreted the equivalent of £25 in dollars in the passport. Certainly possible, he replied, and my 'unlimited' entry and exit visa was available the next day! I just wonder what you may have done!'

The context of my second experience was West Africa – Ghana to be precise. I was staying with a female friend who was a highly professional entrepreneur in the catering and food industry. We were to make a journey across the border into Togo. Before setting off, however, I noticed quite a large number of delicacies being loaded into the back of the car. I enquired what these were for, to which the reply came – wait and see. The border was hugely busy. I was asked to follow her with a bag containing I should think six or seven of these quite large delicacies. As stamps were affixed to the papers and passports, cakes were passed across the table. We were on our way within half an hour of arrival!

Well, amusing though such incidents may seem to be, they do again throw up for us especially in a global context some of the dilemmas posed by operating in quite different social, cultural, national and religious contexts, where the occasional back-hander is more a way of life than it is an ethical or moral problem. I hope, however, as I say, that I have at least been able to demonstrate to you that ethics is indeed relevant to business and that the business of ethics is a very necessary dimension at every level to all those of us who have any interest at all in ensuring the very necessary moral, spiritual and ethical values which enable and encourage the flourishing of a healthy society, people and nation.

One final thought – a cautionary tale if you like – by way of conclusion. A great rabbi once taught this lesson to a successful but unhappy businessman. He took him to the window and asked him, 'What do you see?' The man replied, 'I see the world.' He then took him to a mirror and asked, 'What do you see?' He replied, 'I see myself.' 'That,' said the rabbi, 'is what happens when silver covers glass. Instead of seeing the world you see only yourself.'

A verse of a well-known poem/hymn by the early eighteenth-century English country parson, George Herbert, says the same thing:

> A man that looks on glass,
> on it may stay his eye,
> or if he pleaseth, through it pass
> and then the heavens espy.